Mathematics 9

Exploring the Concepts

T. Anne Yeager

Orangeville, Ontario

Rod Yeager

Orangeville, Ontario

 **McGraw-Hill Ryerson**

Toronto   Montréal   Boston   Burr Ridge, IL   Dubuque, IA   Madison, WI   New York
San Francisco   St. Louis   Bangkok   Bogotá   Caracas   Kuala Lumpur   Lisbon   London   Madrid
Mexico City   Milan   New Delhi   Santiago   Seoul   Singapore   Sydney   Taipei

McGraw-Hill
Ryerson Limited

A Subsidiary of The McGraw·Hill Companies

Mathematics 9
Exploring the Concepts

Copyright © 2002, McGraw-Hill Ryerson Limited, a Subsidiary of The McGraw-Hill Companies. All rights reserved. No part of this publication may be reproduced or transmitted in any form or by any means, or stored in a data base or retrieval system, without the prior written permission of McGraw-Hill Ryerson Limited, or, in the case of photocopying or other reprographic copying, a licence from CANCOPY (Canadian Copyright Licensing Agency), One Yonge Street, Suite 1900, Toronto, Ontario M5E 1E5.

ISBN 0-07-089891-X

http://www.mcgrawhill.ca

3 4 5 6 7 8 9 0   MP   0 9 8 7 6 5 4 3 2

Printed and bound in Canada

Care has been taken to trace ownership of copyright material contained in this text. The publishers will gladly take any information that will enable them to rectify any reference or credit in subsequent printings.

The Geometer's Sketchpad®, Key Curriculum Press, 1150 65th Street, Emeryville, CA 94608, 1-800-995-MATH.
CBL™ and CBR™ are trademarks of Texas Instruments Incorporated.
Graphmatica is shareware distributed by kSoft, Inc. For more information or to download the current version, please visit *http://www.graphmatica.com/*

National Library of Canada Cataloguing in Publication Data

Yeager, T. Anne, date-
   Mathematics 9 : exploring the concepts

ISBN 0-07-089891-X

1. Mathematics-Problems, exercises, etc.-
Juvenile literature. I. Yeager, Rod, date- II. Title.
III. Title: Mathematics nine.

QA39.2.M335 1999   510   C2001-903497-0

PUBLISHER: Diane Wyman
DEVELOPMENTAL EDITOR: Sheila Bassett
SENIOR SUPERVISING EDITOR: Carol Altilia
COPY EDITOR: Frances Schatz
PERMISSIONS EDITOR: Maria DeCambra
EDITORIAL ASSISTANT: Erin Parton
ASSISTANT PROJECT COORDINATORS: Melissa Nippard, Janie Reeson
PRODUCTION SUPERVISOR: Yolanda Pigden
PRODUCTION COORDINATOR: Jennifer Wilkie
INTERIOR DESIGN: Jay Tee Graphics Ltd.
ELECTRONIC PAGE MAKE-UP: Jay Tee Graphics Ltd.
COVER DESIGN: Dianna Little
COVER IMAGE: ©COMSTOCK/Henri Georgi

COPIES OF THIS BOOK
MAY BE OBTAINED BY
CONTACTING:

McGraw-Hill Ryerson Ltd.

WEB SITE:
http://www.mcgrawhill.ca

E-MAIL:
orders@mcgrawhill.ca

TOLL-FREE FAX:
1-800-463-5885

TOLL-FREE CALL:
1-800-565-5758

OR BY MAILING YOUR
ORDER TO:
McGraw-Hill Ryerson
Order Department
300 Water Street
Whitby, ON L1N 9B6

Please quote the ISBN and title when placing your order.

ISBN:
0-07-089891-X

*For our children who taught us that each student
has unique strengths and diverse learning needs,
and that every day is precious.*

Contents

1 Relationships in Mathematics

Data Collection and Analysis

1.1A Data Collection

Collecting data has a purpose or goal. Each time you collect data you will discuss the following questions.

1. What might be the purpose, goal, or use for the data?

2. Who might be interested in an individual piece of collected data? How would it be used?

3. Who might be interested in a **set** of data (either a **census** or a **sample**)? How would it be used?

At this point, you will make a **hypothesis**, collect and organize the data, and make a **conclusion** about your results.
Consider the following questions about the data.

1. What would be the best way to **display** these data?

2. Is a **relationship** or trend evident?

3. Can you use a **mathematical model** to express any relationship? Is this helpful for the purpose of the collection?

4. Are these data **biased** in any way? (Consider sampling, displaying of, questioning or experimental techniques, etc.)

5. a) Can you reach a conclusion?

   b) How could this data collection have been improved?

   c) How else could the data have been displayed?

   d) Was your hypothesis correct? Is there another conclusion possible?

   e) How do the **measures of central tendency** behave?

1.1B   Using Surveys to Gather Data

If you want information on all grade 9 students in your school, you could do a **census survey** (ask every grade 9 student) or do a **sample survey** (ask some of the grade 9 students).

Discuss: Could we use our grade 9 class as a **random sample** to get information about all grade 9 students?

Yes, in some cases, like these: No, in some cases, like these:

1.   1.

2.   2.

3.   3.

Problem

The cafeteria staff is giving all grade 9 students free ice cream bars on Friday. The staff can order vanilla, chocolate, or strawberry ice cream bars. How many bars of each flavour should be ordered?

1.   Discuss this question.

Can you survey the students in your class to find their choice of ice cream flavour and then, use ratios to predict the choice of flavours for all grade 9 students? Explain.

1.1

2. Do a class survey. Record the results of the survey.

Question: What is your choice of ice cream flavour?

Flavour	Tally	Number of Each Flavour Chosen
Chocolate		
Strawberry		
Vanilla		

3. Display the results using a bar, line, or circle graph.

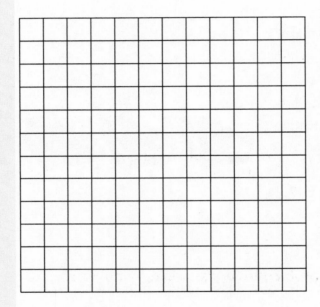 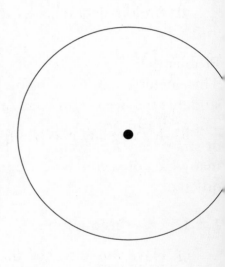

4. Use the results to make a decision.

There are _____ grade 9 students in the school. Thus, the cafeteria staff should order: (show calculations and results)

Vanilla   Chocolate   Strawberry

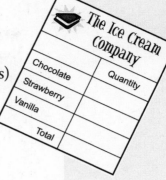

5. Discuss the results.

a) Are the data reliable? Explain.

b) Is there any bias in the survey or the results? Explain.

c) Have you answered the problem that was asked by doing the survey? Explain.

d) Can you think of a way to get better results?

1.1C   Survey Assignment

1. Discuss with your partner this question.
    Can we survey our class about a grade 9 topic of interest?

    Include in your discussion
    • the topic of interest you might survey
    • who would be interested in the results of your survey and why

2. Think of a grade 9 topic of interest that has no more than three
    choices of answers. Survey your class. Record the results of the
    survey.

    Question:

Possible Choices	Tally	Number of Times Chosen

3. Display the results using a bar, line, or circle graph.

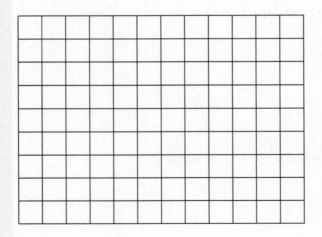

4. Use your results to make a conclusion.
(Explain what you now know about all grade 9 students in your school.)

There are _____ grade 9 students in the school. Thus,

5. Discuss the results.

a) Are the data reliable? Explain.

b) Is there any bias in the survey or the results? Explain.

c) Have you answered the problem that was asked by doing the survey? Explain.

d) Can you think of a way to get better results?

1.1

1.1D Learning Styles Inventory: Personal Results

Complete the Learning Styles Inventory master provided by your teacher before completing this section. Then, base your answers to these questions on the Learning Styles Inventory.

1. What might be the purpose, goal, or use, for these data?

2. **a)** Who might be interested in a single piece of collected data?

    b) How would the data be used?

3. **a)** Who might be interested in a set of data (either from a census or a sample)?

    b) How would the data be used?

    At this point, you will make a **hypothesis, collect** the data, **organize** the data, and then state a **conclusion** about your results.

4. State your hypothesis about your learning style by filling in the blanks.

    I think my learning style is _____

    because _____

5. Record your data from the Learning Styles Inventory you completed before you started this section.

Visual	Auditory	Kinesthetic
V = _____	A = _____	K = _____

6. a) What would be the better way of displaying this data, a bar graph or a circle graph?

1.1

b) Display the data.

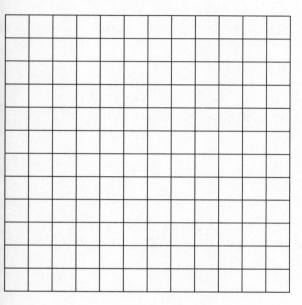
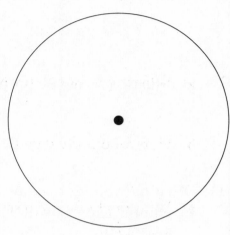

7. Are these data **biased** in any way? Explain. (Consider methods of sampling, displaying, and questioning, or experimental techniques, etc.)

8. a) Was your hypothesis correct?

b) What conclusions can you make?

c) Is there another conclusion possible? Explain.

d) Is this other conclusion better? Explain.

1.1

9. **a)** How could you have improved on the data collection?

    b) How else could you have displayed the data?

10. Refer to questions 1 to 3. Do you think the collection of this information served its purpose? Why?

11. What did you learn about yourself from doing the Learning Styles Inventory? Express your answer in terms of

    • learning at school (classroom work and studying)

    • learning a new activity, such as a sport or game

    • learning how to use an instrument or a tool you have never used before

    • learning about career choices you might make

1.1E   Learning Styles Inventory: Class Results

Complete the Learning Styles Inventory master provided by your teacher before completing this section. Then, base your answers to these questions on the Learning Styles Inventory.

1.   What might be the purpose, goal, or use for these data?

2.   **a)** Who might be interested in a set of data
     (either from a census or from a sample)?

     b) How would the data be used?

At this point, you will make a **hypothesis, collect** data, and then **organize** the data. (A chart on the chalkboard will indicate the individual learning styles of the people in the class.) Finally, you will reach a **conclusion** from the results.

3.   State your hypothesis about the learning style of your class by filling in the blanks.

     I think the primary learning style of the class is

     _____

     because _____

4.   Record your data for the class from the Learning Styles Inventory everyone completed before starting this section.

Visual	Auditory	Kinesthetic
V = _____	A = _____	K = _____

1.1

5. **a)** What would be the better way of displaying this data, a bar graph or a circle graph?

   b) Display the data.

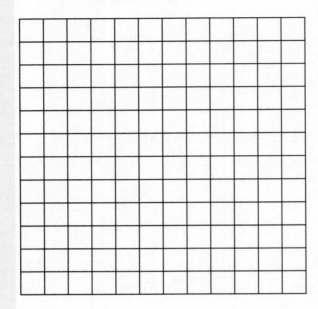 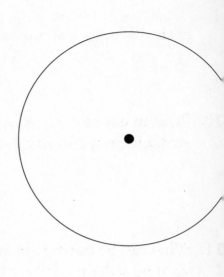

6. Are these data **biased** in any way? Explain. (Consider methods of sampling, displaying, and questioning, or experimental techniques, etc.)

7. Overall conclusions: How could you have improved on the data collection?

8. How else could you have displayed the data?

9. a) Was your hypothesis correct?

b) Is there another conclusion possible? Explain.

c) Is this other conclusion better? Explain.

10. Refer to question 1. Do you think this collecting of information served its purpose? Explain.

11. What can be learned about your class by collecting the results of the learning styles inventory? Express your answer in terms of

- the classroom environment (teaching)

- cooperative learning groups

- learning a new activity or game in class

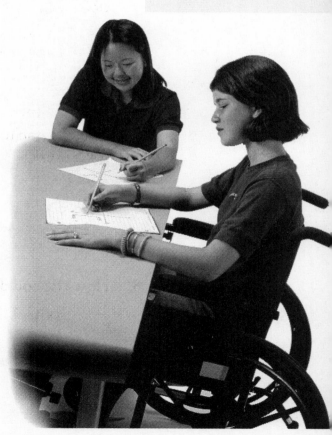

12. a) Compare your learning style inventory results with those of the class. What does this mean?

b) Could you be positively or negatively affected by these results? Explain.

1.1F Drawing a Histogram or Bar Graph on the TI-83 Plus

You can follow these steps to graph a histogram for frequencies of 5, 7, 12, and 2.

1. Set the number of decimal points to 0.
    Press **MODE**.
    Cursor down to **FLOAT**.
    Cursor along to 0. Press **ENTER**.

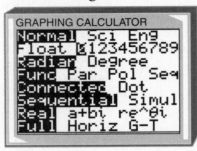

2. Clear all lists.
    Press **MEM** (press **2nd** (yellow key) then +).
    Cursor down to 4 (4:ClrAllLists).
    Press **ENTER**.

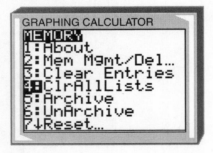

3. Enter the data.
    Press **STAT**.
    Press **ENTER**.

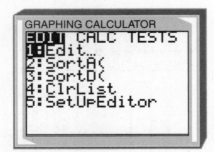

4. Under L1 enter the number for every bar you want (i.e., 1, 2, 3, 4 for 4 bars). (For space between bars use odd numbers i.e., 1, 3, 5, 7). Press **ENTER** after each entry.

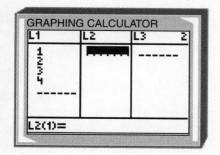 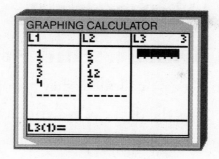

Under L2 enter the frequency for each interval, from your chart. (For example, say that the frequencies are 5, 7, 12, and 2.) Press **ENTER** after each data you enter.
Check the range.

5. Press **WINDOW** (blue key) and enter the values shown in the following calculator screen.

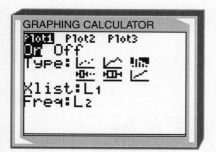

Draw a graph.

6. Press **STAT PLOT** (press **2nd Y=**).
Press **1** (1:Plot1).
Press **ENTER**. Make sure **On** is bold.
Cursor to the bar graph icon. Press **ENTER**.
Set xlist:L1
     Freq:L2   Press **GRAPH** (blue key).

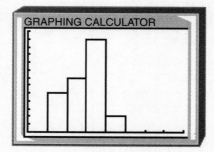

1.1 Completed

Scatter Plots to Show Relationships

1.2A What Is a Scatter Plot?

When data are collected, they are often displayed on a graph.

Sometimes the data can be written as coordinates of points.

When these points are plotted on a grid, the result is called a **scatter plot**.

The scatter plot may, or may not, show that a relationship exists.

Example

You collected data on the height of your corn each week to see if there was a relationship between time and height. The data collected are shown in the table.

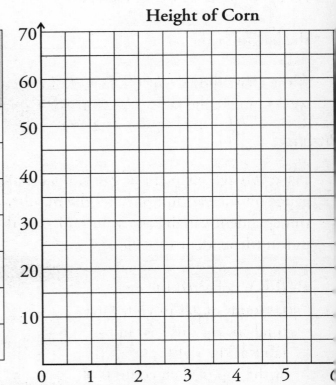

Length of Time (weeks)	Height of Corn (cm)
0	0
1	5
2	18
3	29
4	45
5	59
6	70

Height of Corn

1. Make a scatter plot of the data using the grid above.

   a) Let the horizontal axis represent the time, in weeks. (Write this on your graph.) Time is the **independent variable**.

   b) Let the vertical axis represent the height, in centimetres. (Write this on your graph.) Height is the **dependent variable**.

2. When the data are **continuous**, you can **connect** the points on the scatter plot. When the data are **discrete**, you cannot connect the points on the scatter plot. Does it seem logical to connect the points on your graph in question 1? Explain.

3. Study your graph in question 1. Finish this statement about the relationship between time and height.

   As the number of weeks increases,

   the height of the corn _____

   . If the chart shows that the height of the corn did not change in four weeks, might the farmer be worried? Explain.

Practice

   . Have you ever helped put gas into a car? When you do this, the gas gauge on the gas pump shows the number of litres you have put in (independent variable) to your tank and the total cost of this gas you put in (dependent variable).

   a) If you collected the data (amount of gas in your tank, total cost of this gas) in the table at the right, put a title at the top of each column of this table.

1.2

b) If you were going to graph a scatter plot of the data in the table, how would you label the horizontal axis?

_____

How would you label the vertical axis?

_____

c) Underline the **ordered pair** (points) that could not be on the scatter plot.

(1, $0.749)   (4, $0.15)   (10, $7.79)

d) Describe the finished scatter plot.

e) Would you join the points on the scatter plot? Explain.

2. The data in the table represent the values of a vehicle after different amounts of time.
   a) Construct a scatter plot using the data below.
      Give your graph a title. Label each axis.

Title: _____

Number of Years After Purchase	Approximate Value of the Vehicle ($)
0	28 000
1	24 000
2	21 000
3	18 000
5	14 000
8	9000
10	5000

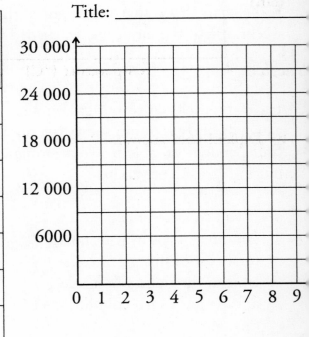

b) Study your scatter plot and then, fill in the blanks.

As the number of years after purchase __increases__

the value of the vehicle _____ .

c) Are the data discrete or continuous? Explain.

d) Discuss with a classmate the factors that might affect the value of a vehicle. List some of the factors other than age.

a) Put some dots on the graph below that might look like a scatter plot of the situation as labelled.

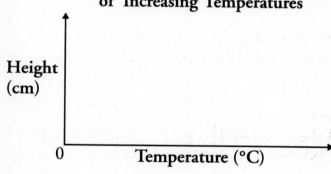

Height of a Snowman After 3 Days of Increasing Temperatures

Height (cm)

0   Temperature (°C)

b) Explain your answer.

1.2B Positive, Negative, or No Correlation?

Positive correlation: If a scatter plot slants upward as you move from left to right, the two variables are said to have a positive correlation. Thus, when one variable increases, the other variable also increases.

Negative correlation: If a scatter plot slants downward as you move from left to the right, the two variables are said to have a negative correlation. Thus, when one variable increases, the other variable decreases.

No correlation: If a scatter plot shows no pattern or clear relationship, the variables are said to have no correlation.

Example 1
This scatter plot shows the height of a tree over several years.

a) Label the axes.

b) Describe the correlation.

c) Complete the following sentence.

As the number of years _____,
the height of the tree increases.

Example 2
This scatter plot shows the number of trees left in a forest as several loggers are cutting them down over a week.

a) Label the axes.

b) Describe the correlation.

c) Complete the following sentence.

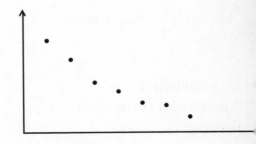

As the number of days increases,
the number of trees left _____.

Example 3

This scatter plot shows the number of questions
students did for math homework compared to the
length of their shoelaces.

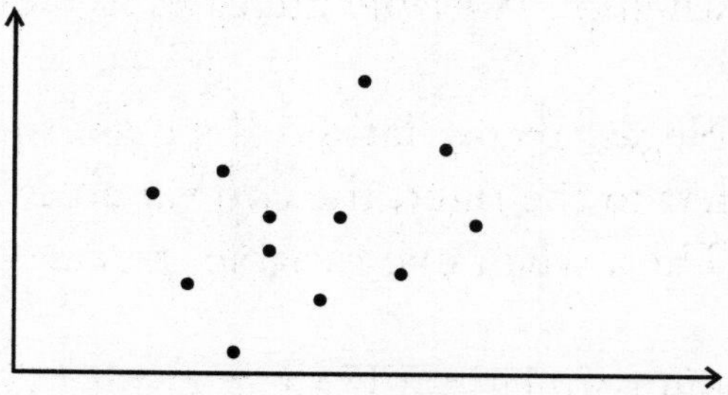

a) Label the axes.

b) Describe the correlation.

_____

c) Describe the relationship in words.

Make up an example of your own. Draw a scatter plot that shows your
example and then complete the sentence.

d) a positive correlation
This is a positive correlation
because

e) a negative correlation
This is a negative correlation
because

f) no correlation
There is no correlation
because

Practice

1.2

1. In each scatter plot, state whether the correlation is positive, negative, or neither. Give reasons for your answers.

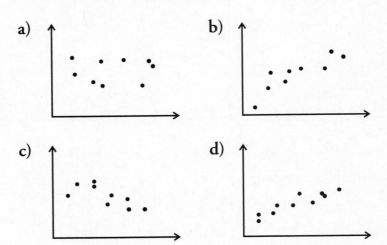

   a)

   b)

   c)

   d)

2. Will each of the following sets of data show a positive correlation, a negative correlation, or no correlation?
   Give reasons for your answers.

   a) the number of pages left to be typed in your essay and the number of pages already typed

   b) the size of a student's hand and the number of rings the student owns

   c) the outside summer temperature and the number of people swimming

1.2

d) the depth of Lake Ontario and the amount of rainfall and snowfall for that year

e) the outside winter temperature and the number of centimetres of ice on Island Lake

f) the energy left in your personal radio batteries and the number of hours you have listened to this radio

g) your take-home pay and the number of hours you work

h) your math mark and the number of hours of studying you do

1.2C Drawing the Line of Best Fit

The line of best fit is a line that approximates the pattern for the data shown in a scatter plot. The line of best fit should be as close as possible to as many of your data points as possible. One purpose of the line of best fit is to help make predictions.

Use scatter plots **A** and **B** below to complete questions 1 to 4.

1. Use a straightedge (clear, if possible) to draw the line of best fit.

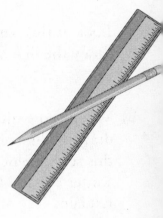

2. Describe how you estimated the line of best fit for each scatter plot.

   A   **B**

3. State the type of correlation for each graph.

   A   **B**

4. Describe a situation that might fit each scatter plot.

   A   **B**

5. **a)** Make up a scatter plot of
      your own.
   b) Ask a classmate to draw a
      line of best fit for your
      scatter plot.
   c) Discuss and identify the
      type of correlation for your
      scatter plot.

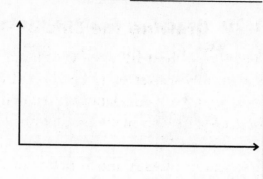

6. **a)** Look at this scatter plot.
      Draw the line of best fit.

   b) Was it more difficult to
      draw the line of best fit for
      this scatter plot than for the
      scatter plots in Question 1?
      Explain.

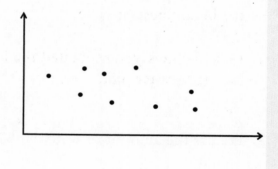

. Compare your line of best fit in question 6 with that of a classmate. Is
it important that all your classmates have lines of best fit that are
identical? Explain.

1.2D Practice: Scatter Plots and Lines of Best Fit

1. **a)** Draw the line of best fit of the data given in
     the diagram.

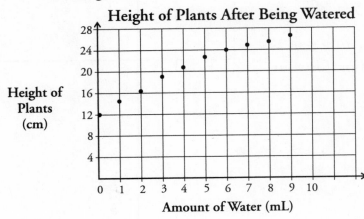

Height of Plants After Being Watered

Height of
Plants
(cm)

Amount of Water (mL)

b) State the relationship in words.

2. Predict the amount of water a plant needs to grow to a height of
     25 cm.

3. Predict the height of plants after getting 5 mL of water.

4. Compare your answers to questions 2 and 3 with those of a partner.
     Explain why your answer might be different from that of your partne

5. a) Make a scatter plot using the data below.

b) Draw the line of best fit.

x Horizontal Axis	y Vertical Axis
9	5
4	18
2	22
4	15
6	15
3	21
8	11
9	10

6. A roofer recorded the number of hours each employee worked in a week and the number of boxes of nails each employee used.

Time (hours)	Number of Boxes of Nails Used
40	24
9	4
19	8
36	28
30	16
28	12
30	14

a) What type of correlation do you think there will be between the time and the number of boxes? Why?

1.2

b) Use the grid to make a scatter plot.

c) Draw the line of best fit.
Did your scatter plot support your answer in part a)?
Explain.

d) Carla plans to work for 21 h this week
doing roofing work.

Estimate how many boxes of nails she
will need.

Note: Looking for an answer within a
graph is called **interpolation**.

e) Estimate the number of hours Joe
worked last week if he used 31 boxes
of nails.

Note: Extending the graph in order to read a number is called
extrapolation.

1.2E Describing Relationships

For each of the following scatter plots,
- circle the words that describe the relationship
- discuss with your partner where you think the line, or curve, of best fit should be. Draw it.
- come up with a situation that could be represented by the graph and the line of best fit shown
- label the axes using the variables of your example

a)

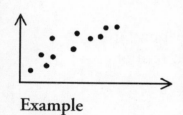

Example

Relationship/no relationship
Positive/negative correlation
Linear/non-linear

b)

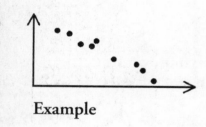

Example

Relationship/no relationship
Positive/negative correlation
Linear/non-linear

c)

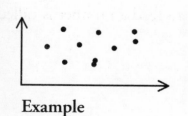

Example

Relationship/no relationship
Positive/negative correlation
Linear/non-linear

d)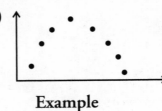

Relationship/no relationship
Positive/negative correlation
Linear/non-linear

Example

e)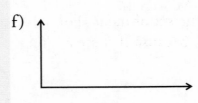

Relationship/no relationship
Positive/negative correlation
Linear/non-linear

Example

f)

In this case, draw your own scatter plot that shows the following.
- Relationship
- Positive correlation
- Non-linear

Example

1.2 Completed

Finding Relationships

1.3A The Hypothesis and the Conclusion

Your **hypothesis** for a relationship must include what you think will be the answers to the following statements.

Your **conclusion** for a relationship must include the answers to the following statements.

1. Does the relationship have a positive, a negative, or no correlation?

2. Describe the relationship in question 1? Use variables. (For example, as the number of books *increases*, the mass *increases*. Therefore, the relationship has a positive correlation.)

3. Is the relationship linear or non-linear?

4. Is the origin, (0, 0), a reasonable element of the set of data? (For example, the origin, (0, 0), is one of the data, because if there are no books, there is no mass.)

5. Is the relationship **discrete** or **continuous**?

Using the data collected or provided, make a scatter plot and join the points using either a **curve** or **line of best fit**.

Check your hypothesis and restate each item in your conclusion (report).

1.3B Cooling Temperature vs. Time

Make a hypothesis about the temperature of the boiling water in the cup over a period of time (say, 40 minutes).

Include the answers to all 5 questions from Section 1.3A on page 31 of this book.

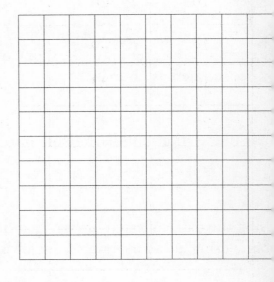

☞

☞

☞

☞

☞

Complete the following chart with the data you collected in class. Graph the points in your table.

Time (minutes)	Temperature (°C)
0	
5	

Make one or more conclusions.

1.3C Can You Find a Relationship?

One purpose of finding a relationship is to make conclusions or predictions.

You are going to collect some data from your friends, draw the graph, and see if a relationship exists.

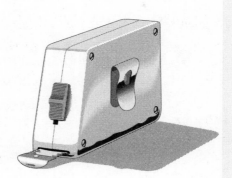

Part A

1. Fill out the table by gathering the data from your classmates. Measure carefully.

Hand Span (Hand Stretched Out) (cm)	Forearm Length (from Tip of Finger to Elbow) (cm)	Length of Time You Watch TV in a Week (minutes)	Shoe Length (Toe to Heel) (cm)	Length of Leg (Heel to Knee) (cm)
10	20	60	12	24
18	26	0	19	27
12	23	30	18	35
25	45	100	35	60

1.3

2. Choose any two columns above.
   a) Do you think there is a connection between the data in them? For example, do you think that there is a positive correlation between shoe length and forearm length? That is, a longer shoe length would mean a longer forearm length?

   b) Make a hypothesis about any relationship between the data in the two columns you chose.

   Hypothesis

   ☞

   ☞

   ☞

   ☞

   ☞

3. Use the grid at the right to make a scatter plot of the data you chose. Give the graph a title and label the axes carefully.

4. a) Was your hypothesis correct?

   b) Adjust your hypothesis, if necessary, and make a final conclusion.

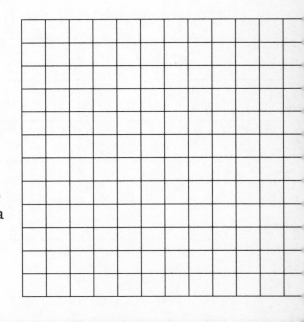

Name ______________________ Date ______________

5. a) Make up a question that can be solved using your graph. For example, what is the likely shoe length for someone whose forearm is 40 cm long?

b) Answer your question.

Part B

1. Choose two columns from your table of data that are different from those in the previous exercise. Make a hypothesis about any relationship you think there is between the two columns you chose.

Hypothesis

☞

☞

☞

☞

☞

2. Use the grid at the right to make a scatter plot of the data you chose. Give the graph a title, and label the axes carefully.

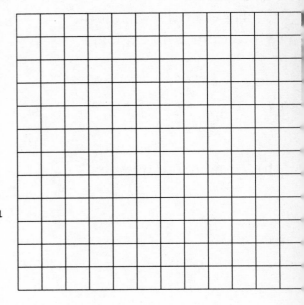

3. a) Was your hypothesis correct?

b) Adjust your hypothesis, if necessary, and make a conclusion.

4. a) Make up a question that can be solved using your graph. For example, what is the likely shoe length for someone whose forearm is 40 cm long?

b) Answer your question.

Part C

1. Choose two columns from your table of data that are different from any other pair of columns in the previous exercises.
Make a hypothesis about any relationship you think there is between the data in the two columns you chose.

Hypothesis

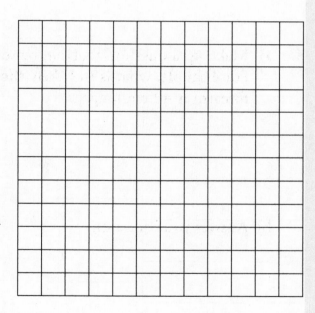

☞

☞

☞

☞

☞

2. Use the grid at the right to make a scatter plot of the data you chose. Give the graph a title, and label the axes carefully.

3.
  a) Was your hypothesis correct?
  b) Adjust your hypothesis, if necessary, and make a conclusion.

4.
  a) Make up a question that can be solved using your graph. For example, what is the likely shoe length for someone whose forearm is 40 cm long?

  b) Answer your question.

1.3D Investigation: Finding Relationships

Experiment _____

1. Make a hypothesis about the relationship.

    ☞

    ☞

    ☞

    ☞

    ☞

2. With your group, go to the assigned station and investigate your
    hypothesis by gathering and organizing data.

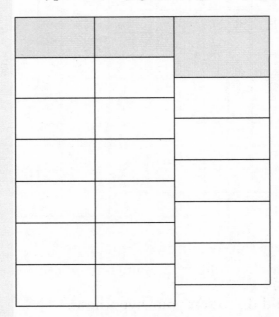
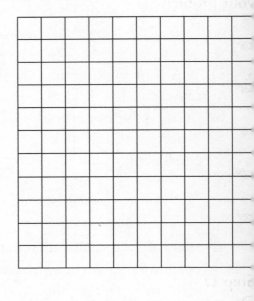

    After collecting the data, complete questions 3 to 5.
3. Create a scatter plot of your relation.
4. Draw the line or curve of best fit.
5. Discuss your graph with your group and record the relationship.
    Refer to your hypothesis and your graph.

1.3E Make an Experiment of Your Own

1.3

Step A
With your group, choose one of the following problems.

1. Does the number of successful foul shots that a person makes depend on the person's height?
2. Does the rebound height of a ball change depending on the height from which it is dropped?
3. Does the time it takes for an object to fall a certain distance depend on its mass?
4. Write a problem of your choice. (Have your teacher approve it.)

Step B
Identify the variables involved in your problem.

Step C
State a hypothesis that describes the relationship you believe exists for your problem:

☞

☞

☞

☞

☞

Step D
Describe an experiment that you could do to test your hypothesis. Include the materials required and the number of trials you think are needed.

Step E
Perform your experiment and gather your data. Fill out a chart and draw the graph.

Step F
Make conclusions by referring to your data and graph.

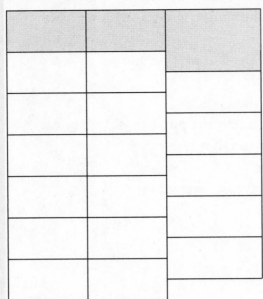 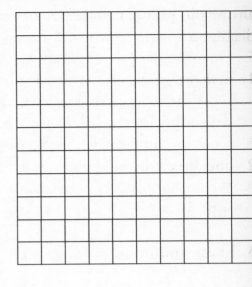

Rewrite any parts of your hypothesis that are untrue.

Step G
Can you think of any ways to improve upon your experiment? Explain why you believe these changes would improve your results.

Step H
Think of 2 questions that can be answered using the results of your experiment. Answer the questions.

-

-

1.3F Summary Page and Journal

1.3

What have you learned about each of the following? Express your
answers in words, using correct mathematical language. You may use
diagrams to help explain your answers.

1. scatter plots

2. line of best fit

3. linear/non-linear relation

4. positive/negative/no correlation

5. discrete/continuous data

6. What must a good hypothesis include?

☞

☞

☞

☞

☞

1.3 Completed

Is It Really Linear?

It is important to know for sure when a relationship is linear and when it is not. Looking at a scatter plot to make this decision is not always accurate. If you are sure a relationship is linear, you can express it as an equation, and make accurate predictions.

1.4A Expressions Involving Integers

Multiplying and Dividing Integers

1. Complete the multiplication chart and look for a pattern.

×	6	2	0	−3	−5	−10
4						
1						
0						
−1						
−3						

Conclusions

Which word, positive or negative, makes each statement true?

*   When multiplying or dividing 2 positive numbers, the result

    is a _____ number.

*   When multiplying or dividing 2 negative numbers, the result

    is a _____ number.

*   When multiplying or dividing a positive number and a

    negative number, the result is a _____ number.

Practice

1. Calculate.

a) $(7)(3) = $ _____

b) $(2)(-4) = $ _____

c) $(-3)(-5) = $ _____

d) $(-1)(7) = $ _____

e) $(4) \div (2) = $ _____

f) $(-9) \div (3) = $ _____

g) $(12) \div (-6) = $ _____

h) $(-100) \div (-10) = $ _____

2. A negative sign in front of a bracket means multiply by (-1).

Calculate $-(-9) = $ $-(8) = $

Adding and Subtracting Integers

A positive number means "going up" on the thermometer; a negative number means "going down" on the thermometer. Always begin at 0 and move up or down, as shown by the + or − sign.

Practice

. Calculate.

a) $4 - 5 = $

b) $-2 + 5 = $

c) $-3 - 4 = $

d) $5 + 2 = $

e) $-8 + 0 = $

f) $-6 - 6 = $

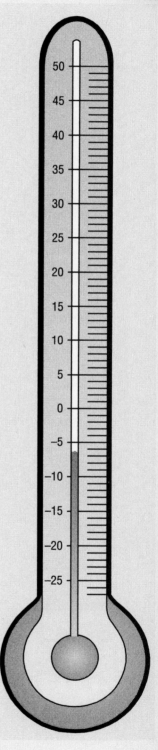

1.4

When you have adjacent signs, use your rules for the multiplication of signs to reduce the signs to only one. Then, move up and down the thermometer.

Example 1

$-(-3) + 4$
$= 3 + 4$
$= 7$

Example 2

$3 - (-5)$
$= 3 + 5$
$= 8$

2. Calculate.

a) $5 - 7 =$

b) $8 - 3 =$

c) $-7 - 2 =$

d) $-6 + (-3) =$

e) $7 - (-2) =$

f) $3 + (-9) =$

g) $5 - (-3) =$

h) $-3 - (-5) =$

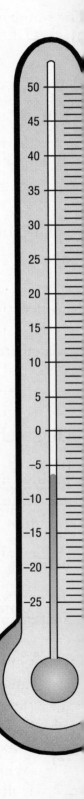

1.4B Relationships and First Differences

Predict whether the following relationship is linear or non-linear.

The number of pens purchased and the total cost, if each pen costs $1.50.

Data

Number of Pens	Total Cost ($)	First Difference
1	1.50	
2	3.00	
3	4.50	
4	6.00	
5	7.50	
6	9.00	
7	10.50	

Graph of Relationship

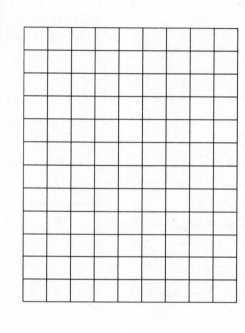

1. Draw a graph of the relationship.
2. Was your prediction correct?
3. Every entry in the first difference column is _____ .

   This is always true if the relationship is _____ .

   Be sure your independent variable always increases by equal increments.

4. a) Go to pages 38 and 40. Make use of the third column of each table by finding the first differences for each investigation, where the independent variable increases by equal increments.
   b) Check if each relationship is linear (values in the first difference column are the same, or very close), or non-linear (values in the first difference column are not the same). Is this consistent with each graph?

1.4C Practice: First Differences

For each set of data, determine the first differences. Use the space at the right of the table to explain how to use this result to determine if the relationship is linear or non-linear, and if it is a positive or a negative correlation.

x	y	First Difference
1	6	
		12 – 6 = 6
2	12	
		18 – 12 = 6
3	18	
		24 – 18 =
4	24	
5	30	
6	36	

Explanation:
In each case, the independent variable, x, increases by the same amount (+1), and the dependent variable, y, increases by the same amount (+6).

Conclusion:
The relationship is linear and a positive correlation.

x	y	First Difference
4	80	
		60 – 80 = –20
6	60	
8	40	
10	20	
12	0	
14	–20	

Explanation:

Conclusion:

Name _____   Date _____

Remember, the increments for the independent variable, x, must be equal.

x	y	First Difference
4	30	
8	40	
12	60	
16	90	
20	130	
24	180	

Explanation:

Conclusion:

x	y	First Difference
1	100	
3	140	
5	180	
7	220	
11	300	
13	340	
15	380	

Explanation:

Conclusion:

1.4

Remember, the increments for the independent variable, x, must be equal.

x	y	First Difference
50	2.5	
60	3	
70	3.5	
90	4.5	
100	5	
120	6	
130	6.5	

Explanation:

Conclusion:

x	y	First Difference
1	1	
2	−2	
3	3	
4	−4	
5	5	
6	−6	
7	7	

Explanation:

Conclusion:

1.4 Completed

Combination Relationships

1.5A More Relationships

Relationships can be linear. This means:

Relationships can be non-linear. This means:

Relationships can have a positive correlation. This means:

Relationships can have a negative correlation. This means:

Relationships can be a combination of the above. This means:

Insert titles on the axes of each of the following graphs.

. Graph the number of leaves on a maple tree
  throughout the year, starting in January and
  ending in December.

2. Graph your hunger level throughout the day, starting at 08:00 and ending at 21:00.

3. Graph your distance from home throughout a typical school day.

4. Graph the height of a sunflower in the garden, from germination in the spring to diedown in the winter.

5. Make up an example of your own. Graph it and explain it to a classmate. Show where the correlation is linear, non-linear, and positive and negative.

1.5B A Picture Goes With the Story

Several students left home to go to school. They each had a story to tell about their trip to school. Explain why each story goes with the picture.

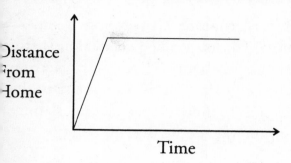

Amir quickly rides his bike to school and then waits there for his friends.

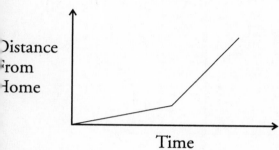

Sandu walks slowly to school for the first half of the distance, and then runs the rest of the distance.

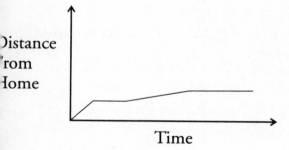

Chris runs to the corner, waits for his friend, walks the rest of the distance, and then stops and talks to his friends.

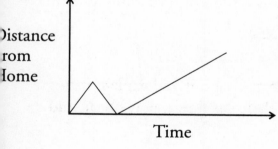

Sara runs to a neighbour's, realizes she forgot her homework, and runs home to collect it. Then, she jogs the whole distance to school.

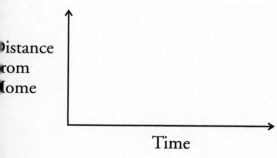

Draw the picture for Myrna. Myrna leaves home on her bike. At about the three-quarter distance mark, she hits the curb and gets a flat tire. She tries to fix the tire, but in the end, has to push her bike to school.

1.5C Graphs That Represent a Story

For each of the following, draw a graph that represents the story.

1. On Monday, the warehouse for L Mart Stores is open from 7 a.m. until 3 p.m. At 7 a.m., it is empty. Trucks, arriving continuously from 7 a.m. to 11 a.m., fill the warehouse to about 75% capacity. Starting at 12 noon, and for 2 h, trucks take stock from the warehouse to the stores. Again, from 2 p.m. until closing time, trucks take stock from the warehouse to the stores until the warehouse is again empty.

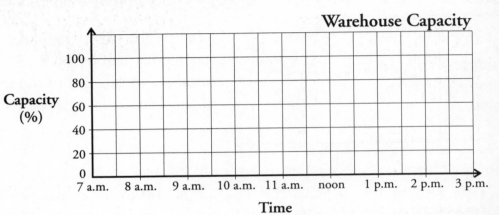

2. The following graph represents the number of cans of pop in a vending machine during one school day. Make up a story for the following graph. Be specific about times and amounts in your story. Make your story interesting and realistic.

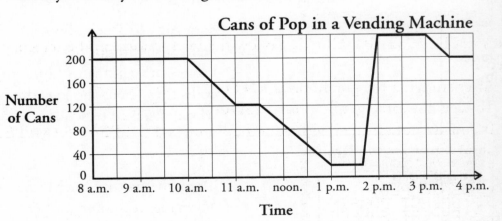

Story

1.5D CBL™/CBR™ Data Collection and Graphs

You will need a CBR™ motion detector and a TI-83 Plus graphing calculator with connecting cable.

Step 1 The Ranger Program
- Connect the calculator and the CBR™ using the cable.
- Turn on the calculator.
- Press **APPS** (blue key).
- Press **2** (2: CBL™/CBR™).
- Press **ENTER**.
- Press **3** (3: RANGER).

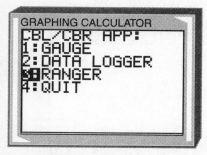

Press **ENTER**. (You are at the main menu.)
  *Press **2** (2: SET DEFAULTS).

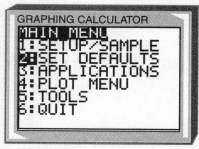

Press **ENTER** (START NOW). Follow the instructions on the screen.

Step 2
- After studying the graph, press **ENTER**.
- To view the same graph, press **1** (SHOW PLOT).
- If you are not satisfied with your graph, press **3** (REPEAT SAMPLE).

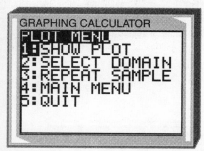

For the next sample, press **4** (MAIN MENU) and repeat from the *
in Step 1 above.

1.5E Take a Walk and Tell the Story

Part A
- A story is described in each question.
- In the screen at the left, draw the graph that you think describes the story.
- Check your answer with the CBR™ by walking the story. In the screen at the right, sketch what you see on your CBR™ screen.

1. Begin 4 m from a wall. Walk toward the wall. When you are 0.5 m from the wall run backward to the starting position. Stop.

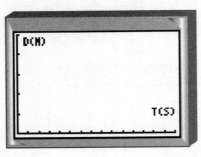 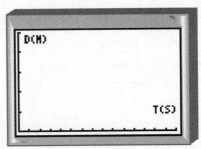

2. Begin 4 m from a wall. Walk toward the wall for 4 s. Stop for 5 s. Run backward to your starting position. Stop.

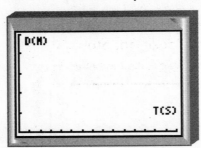 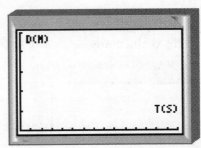

3. Begin at the wall. Walk *slowly* backward until you are 5 m from the wall. Then walk *slowly* toward the wall. Stop.

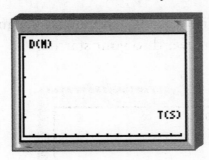 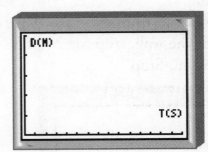

4. Begin 4 m from the wall. Walk toward the wall for 3 s. Stop for 4 s. Walk slowly until you are 0.5 m from the wall. Run backward to the starting position. Stop.

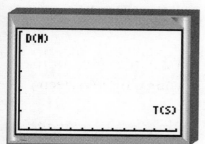
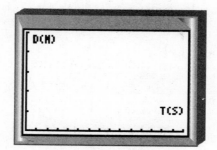

. Begin at the wall. Run backward for 3 s. Stop for 5 s. Walk forward to the starting position. Stop.

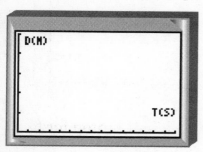
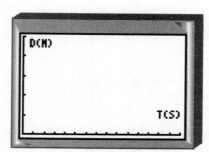

. Begin 5 m from the wall. Walk toward the wall. When you are 0.5 m from the wall, walk backward to the starting position. Stop.

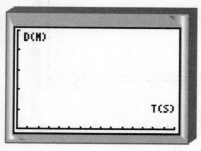
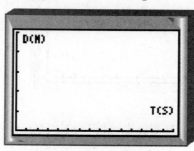

. Begin 5 m from the wall. Walk toward the wall. When you are 0.5 m from the wall, stop for 2 s. Then, run backward to your starting position. Stop.

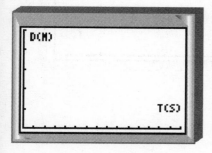
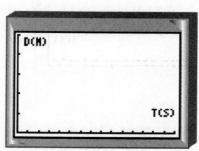

Part B

A graph is shown for each question.

- Tell the story that you think describes the graph.
- Check your answer with the CBR™ by walking the story.

1. The graph.

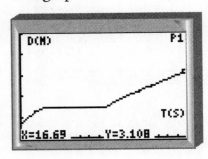

Story

CBR™ graph of your story.

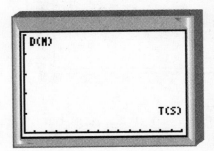

2. The graph.

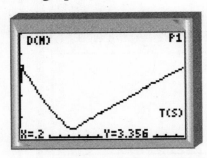

Story

CBR™ graph of your story.

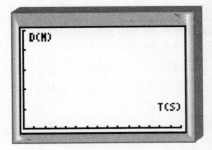

3. The graph.   CBR™ graph of your story.

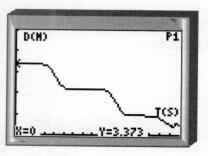   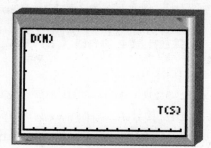

Story

4. Draw your own graph.

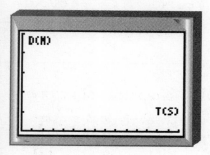   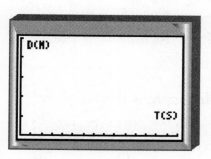

Story

1.5 Completed

Rates of Change

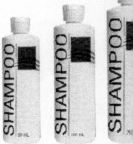

1.6A Estimate and Calculate Unit Rates

For each question,
- do one digit estimation and show your work
- ask yourself if the answer is reasonable
- use your calculator to check your answer
- answer any further questions

1. Shampoo comes in small, medium, and large sizes.

	Small 50 mL for $2.19	Medium 100 mL for $3.79	Large 200 mL for $5.49
Estimate.			
Is my answer reasonable?	Yes/No	Yes/No	Yes/No
Unit cost for each size.			

Which size is the best buy?

2. The BIG G Restaurant sells small, regular, and large burgers.

	Small 45 g for $1.29	Regular 80 g for $1.79	Large 150 g for $2.89
Estimate.			
Is my answer reasonable?	Yes/No	Yes/No	Yes/No
Unit cost for each size.			

Which size is the best buy?

Why might some people not purchase the best buy?

3. Paint can be purchased in a sample size, a 1-L size can and a 4-L can size.

	Sample 125 mL for $3.99	1 L paint $12.19	4 L for $28.79
Estimate.			
Is my answer reasonable?	Yes/No	Yes/No	Yes/No
Unit cost for each size.			

Which size is the best buy?

Why might you purchase a 1-L can rather than a 4-L can?

4. CD Club A gives you 3 CDs when you join, plus 10 more for $65.00. CD Club B gives you 6 CDs when you join, plus 5 more for $55.00.

	CD Club A	CD Club B
Estimate.		
Is my answer reasonable?	Yes/No	Yes/No
Unit cost for each CD.		

What things other than cost might you consider if you join a CD Club?

1.6B Rates of Change

Think of an object that is shaped like a disk. Make a hypothesis about the number of disks and the total length when lined up end to end.

Hypothesis:

☞

☞

☞

☞

☞

Gather and Record Data

1. Fill out the table, and find the **first differences**.
2. On the graph on the following page, make a **scatter plot** showing the number of disks lined up end to end and their total length.
3. Draw the **line of best fit** for each type of disk. Use a different colour of line for each type of disk.

Type of Disk: _____				Type of Disk: _____		
Number of Disks	Total Length (cm)	First Difference		Number of Disks	Total Length (cm)	First Difference
1				1		
2				2		
3				3		
4				4		
5				5		

Type of Disk: _____		
Number of Disks	Total Length (cm)	First Difference
1		
2		
3		
4		
5		

Type of Disk: _____		
Number of Disks	Total Length (cm)	First Difference
1		
2		
3		
4		
5		

4. **a)** Observe the graphs of the different types of disks. What do you notice?

b) Discuss the steepness of the lines.

a) Study the first differences for the each type of disks. Describe what you notice.

b) Relate the above to the **slope of the line** and the **rate of change**.

1.6 Completed

Name _____   Date _____

These awards are to help you keep track of your successes in the grade 9 applied course. Your teacher will instruct you as to how you will use them. Keep up the good work.

Congratulations

1.1 Completed on
_____

Signatures_____
_____

Comments:

Achievement:
Thinking/Inquiry: 1, 2, 3, 4, NA
Communication: 1, 2, 3, 4, NA
Knowledge: 1, 2, 3, 4, NA
Application: 1, 2, 3, 4, NA

Congratulations

1.2 Completed on
_____

Signatures_____
_____

Comments:

Achievement:
Thinking/Inquiry: 1, 2, 3, 4, NA
Communication: 1, 2, 3, 4, NA
Knowledge: 1, 2, 3, 4, NA
Application: 1, 2, 3, 4, NA

Congratulations

1.3 Completed on
_____

Signatures_____
_____

Comments:

Achievement:
Thinking/Inquiry: 1, 2, 3, 4, NA
Communication: 1, 2, 3, 4, NA
Knowledge: 1, 2, 3, 4, NA
Application: 1, 2, 3, 4, NA

Congratulations

1.4 Completed on
_____

Signatures_____
_____

Comments:

Achievement:
Thinking/Inquiry: 1, 2, 3, 4, NA
Communication: 1, 2, 3, 4, NA
Knowledge: 1, 2, 3, 4, NA
Application: 1, 2, 3, 4, NA

Name _____   Date _____

Congratulations

1.5 Completed on

_____

Signatures_____

_____

Comments:

Achievement:
Thinking/Inquiry: 1, 2, 3, 4, NA
Communication: 1, 2, 3, 4, NA
Knowledge: 1, 2, 3, 4, NA
Application: 1, 2, 3, 4, NA

Congratulations

1.6 Completed on

_____

Signatures_____

_____

Comments:

Achievement:
Thinking/Inquiry: 1, 2, 3, 4, NA
Communication: 1, 2, 3, 4, NA
Knowledge: 1, 2, 3, 4, NA
Application: 1, 2, 3, 4, NA

2 Algebra and Relations

Exponents

2.1A Exponents: Introduction

1. a) Take a sheet of paper. Into how many sections
        is the sheet divided?   _____

    b) Fold the sheet of paper in half and open it.
        Now, how many sections are there? _____

    c) Fold the sheet of paper in half again and open it.
        Now, how many sections are there? _____

    d) Continue in this fashion, filling out the chart as you go.

Number of Times Folded Into Halves	Total Number of Sections	$2^{\text{number of times folded}}$ = number of sections
0		
1		
2		
3		
4		
5		
6		

2. Describe the relationship in
    question 1. Then, graph it on
    the grid.

3. Use the pattern established
    and/or your graph to predict
    the number of sections.

    a) after 8 folds

        _____

        (2^8 =   )

    b) after 10 folds

        _____

        (2^{10} =   )

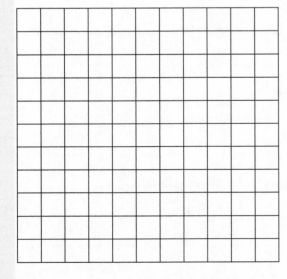

4. Repeat question 1, but this time fold the sheet of paper in thirds and then open it.

a) How many sections are there after the first folding? _____

b) How many sections are there after the second folding? _____

c) How many sections are there after the third folding? _____

2.1

d) Continue in this fashion, filling out the chart as you go.

Number of Times Folded Into Thirds	Total Number of Sections	$3^{\text{number of times folded}}$ = number of sections
0		
1		
2		
3		
4		
5 (You may need to predict here.)		
6 (You may need to predict here.)		

5. Describe the relationship in question 4. Then, graph it on the grid.

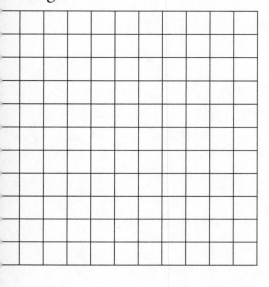

6. Use the pattern established and/or your graph to predict the number of sections.

a) after 8 folds

_____

$(3^8 =)$

b) after 10 folds

_____

$(3^{10} =)$

Exponents in the Real World: Exponential Growth

Some bacteria multiply by *doubling* every hour. This is called **exponential growth**. The graphs of these relationships are called **exponential graphs**. Fill in the blanks in Example 1.

Example 1

You have 50 of this type of bacteria at the start.

After 1 hour there are
$50(2)^1 = 50(2)$
$\qquad = 100$ bacteria

After 2 h there are
$50(2)^2 = 50(4)$
$\qquad = 200$ bacteria

After 3 h there are
$50(2)^3 = 50(\quad)$
$\qquad = \underline{\quad}$ bacteria

After 4 h there are
$50(2)^{\underline{\quad}} = 50(\quad)$
$\qquad = \underline{\quad}$ bacteria

After _____ h there are $50(2)^7 = 50(\quad)$
$\qquad\qquad\qquad = \underline{\quad\quad}$ bacteria

After n hours there are _____ bacteria.

Some insects multiply by *tripling* every hour. Fill in the blanks in Example 2.

Example 2

You have 10 such insects at the start.

After 1 h there are
$10(3)^1 = 10(3)$
$\qquad = 30$ insects

After 2 h there are
$10(3)^2 = 10(\quad)$
$\qquad = \underline{\quad}$ insects

After 3 h there are
$10(3)^{\underline{\quad}} = 10(\quad)$
$\qquad = \underline{\quad}$ insects

After _____ hours there are
$10(\quad)^{\underline{\quad}} = 10(\quad)$
$\qquad = 810$ insects

After n h there are $10(3)^{\underline{\quad}} = \underline{\quad}$ insects.

Can you think of other examples of exponential growth?

2.1B Understanding Powers: Exponent Rules

Multiplication of Powers

Example 1

5^3 means $5 \times 5 \times 5$

5^4 means $5 \times 5 \times 5 \times 5$

Power ⟶ 5^3 ⟵ Exponent / Base

Thus, $5^3 \times 5^4$ means _____ × _____ = 5^7

Example 2

2^5 means _____

2^3 means _____

Thus, $2^5 \times 2^3$ means _____ × _____ = _____

Explain the rule for multiplication of powers with the same base by filling in the blanks.

To multiply powers with the _____ _____, you must

_____ the exponents and _____ the base the same.

$$\boxed{\text{In general: } (x^a)(x^b) = x^{a+b}}$$

Practice

. Use this rule to simplify each of the following.

a) $3^4 \times 3^8 =$ b) $7^6 \times 7^4 =$ c) $4^7 \times 4^6 =$

d) $8^{20} \times 8^9 =$ e) $5^7 \times 5^{-2} =$ f) $3^{-6} \times 3^7 =$

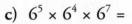

2. Use this rule to simplify each of the following.

a) $2^5 \times 2^4 \times 2^6 =$

b) $5^4 \times 5^4 \times 5^5 =$

c) $6^5 \times 6^4 \times 6^7 =$

d) $2^5 \times 3^4 \times 2^6 =$

e) $2^5 \times 3^4 \times 4^6 =$

f) $2^{-5} \times 2^4 \times 2^6 =$

3. Use this rule to simplify each of the following.

a) $2^5 \times 2^{-3} \times 2^2 \times 2^{-1} =$

b) $2^5 \times 3^3 \times 2^2 \times 3^1 =$

c) $5^6 \times 5^3 \times 2^2 \times 2^1 =$

d) $3^5 \times 2^3 \times 3^2 \times 2^{-1} =$

e) $4^5 \times 4^{-3} \times 4^2 \times 2^1 =$

f) $2^5 \times 3^3 \times 4^2 \times 2^{-1} =$

Division of Powers

Example 1

5^6 means $5 \times 5 \times 5 \times 5 \times 5 \times 5$

5^4 means $5 \times 5 \times 5 \times 5$

Thus, $5^6 \div 5^4$ means _____ =

Example 2

2^8 means _____

2^3 means _____

Thus, $2^5 \div 2^3$ means _____ =

Explain the rule for division of powers with the same base, by filling in the blanks.

To divide powers with the _____ _____, you must

_____ the exponents and _____ the base the same.

$$\boxed{\text{In general: } x^a \div x^b = x^{a-b}}$$

Practice

Use this rule to simplify the following.

a) $3^9 \div 3^8 =$ b) $2^5 \div 2^4 =$

c) $7^6 \div 7^4 =$ d) $5^4 \div 5^4 =$

e) $4^7 \div 4^6 =$ f) $6^5 \div 6^{-4} =$

g) $8^{20} \div 8^9 =$ h) $2^5 \div 3^4 =$

i) $5^7 \div 5^{-2} =$ j) $3^{16} \div 3^7 =$

Power of a Power
Complete the following examples.

Example 1
$(5^6)^3$ means $5^6 \times 5^6 \times 5^6$

$= (5 \times 5 \times 5 \times 5 \times 5 \times 5)(5 \times 5 \times 5 \times 5 \times 5 \times 5)(5 \times 5 \times 5 \times 5 \times 5 \times 5)$

$=$

Thus, $(5^6)^3 =$

2.1

Example 2
$(2^3)^4$ means $2^3 \times 2^3 \times 2^3 \times 2^3$

$= (2 \times 2 \times 2)(2 \times 2 \times 2)(2 \times 2 \times 2)(2 \times 2 \times 2)$

$=$

Thus, $(2^3)^4 =$

Explain the rule for the power of a power by filling in the blanks.

To raise a power to an exponent, _____ the exponents

and _____ the base the same.

$$\boxed{\text{In general: } (x^a)^b = x^{ab}}$$

Practice
Use this rule to simplify the following.

a) $(2^3)^5 =$ _____

    $=$ _____

b) $(3^3)^4 =$ _____

    $=$ _____

c) $(4^3)^7 =$ _____

    $=$ _____

d) $(2^6)^4 =$ _____

    $=$ _____

e) $(5^3)^9 =$ _____

    $=$ _____

f) $(2^3)^4(2^2)^4 =$ _____

    $=$ _____

g) $(3^4)^4(5^3)^5 =$ _____

    $=$ _____

h) $(2^{-3})^{-4}(2^3)^2 =$ _____

    $=$ _____

2.1C Powers With Variables

Variables in a power, such as those in a base or an exponent, follow the same rules as those for numbers. **No new rules!!!**

Simplify in Examples 1 to 3.

Example 1

$x^5 = (x)(x)(x)(x)(x)$ $x^3 = (x)(x)(x)$

Thus, $(x^5)(x^3) = (x)(x)(x)(x)(x)(x)(x)(x)$

$\qquad\qquad = x^8$

Recall the rule for multiplying powers by completing this sentence.

When multiplying powers of the same base,

_____

Example 2

$x^8 \div x^3 =$ _____ ÷ _____

$\qquad =$ _____

Recall the rule for dividing powers by completing the sentence.

When dividing powers of the same base,

_____

Example 3

$(x^3)^5 =$ _____

$\qquad =$ _____

$\qquad =$ _____

Recall the rule for finding the power of a power by completing the sentence.

When finding a power of a power,

_____

$$\text{In general: } x^a x^b = x^{a+b}, \ \frac{x^a}{x^b} = x^{a-b}, \ (x^a)^b = x^{ab}$$

2.1

Practice

1. Simplify each of the following.

   a) $x^7 x^3 =$ **b)** $x^5 \div x^2 =$

   c) $c^5 \div c^{-2} =$ **d)** $y^4 y^7 =$

   e) $m^4 \div m^2 =$ **f)** $(m^5)^4 =$

   g) $n^3 n^6 b^4 b^7 =$ **h)** $z^3 s^4 z^1 s^4 =$

   i) $(m^{-5})^{-2} =$ **j)** $(q^6)^2 \div (q^4) =$

   k) $2^3 x^{-4} 2^4 x^5 =$ **l)** $v^6 b^{-2} v^2 b^6 =$

2. Make up a few questions of your own, similar to those in question 1. Be sure to include questions involving all three exponent rules. Exchange your questions with those of a classmate and simplify them. Check their answers.

   a)   **b)**

   c)   **d)**

   e)   **f)**

2.1D The Negative Exponent: What Is It?

Answer 1 Look for a Pattern

Mathematics follows patterns. Fill in the chart. Use what you already know about exponents, and follow the pattern established.

Power	2^4	2^3	2^2	2^1	2^0	2^{-1}	2^{-2}	2^{-3}	2^{-4}
Value									

Conclusion   A power with a negative exponent is

Answer 2 Use Algebra

The rule you learned for the division of powers is true for all numbers. (Do you remember it?) If you use this rule in the following problem you get

$$2^5 \div 2^8$$
$$= 2^{5-8}$$
$$= 2^{-3}$$

If you do this same problem using the basic rules of arithmetic you get

$$2^5 \div 2^8$$

$$= \frac{2 \times 2 \times 2 \times 2 \times 2}{2 \times 2 \times 2 \times 2 \times 2 \times 2 \times 2 \times 2}$$

$$= \frac{1}{2 \times 2 \times 2}$$

$$= \frac{1}{2^3}$$

You used two correct mathematical methods to solve this problem. This means that the two answers must be equivalent.

Thus, $2^{-3} = \frac{1}{2^3}$.

Write the conclusion in your own words.

Answer 3 Use Technology and Graphing

You could graph $y = 2^x$ using positive values for x, and then extrapolate this graph for negative values of x. A good way to do this is to use technology, such as a graphing calculator.

- To set the number of decimal places to 5, press **MODE**. Cursor down and along to 5. Press **ENTER**.

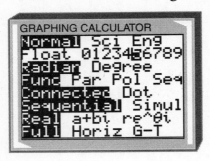

- Press **WINDOW**. Set Xmin=–5, Xmax=5, Ymin=–5, Ymax=50.

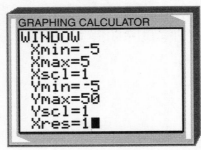

- Graph $y = 2^x$.

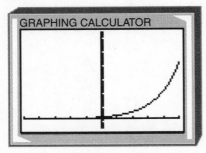

- Use the **TRACE** and the **ZOOM** to find values of y for values of x between –5 and 0.

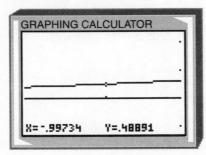

1. From your calculator, read off the values for these powers. Round your answers to two decimal places.

   a) 2^{-5}

   b) 2^{-4}

   c) 2^{-3}

   d) 2^{-2}

   e) 2^{-1}

   f) 2^{0}

2. Express each answer in question 1 as a power of 2 with a positive exponent. See answer 2 on page 75 of this book.

3. Write a rule for writing powers with negative exponents as powers with positive exponents.
   Conclusion

4. Express each power with a positive exponent.

   a) 4^{-2}

   b) 3^{-3}

   c) x^{-5}

   d) $\left(\dfrac{1}{2}\right)^{-3}$

   e) 5^{-2}

   f) $3^{-1} \times 2^{-2}$

5. Use your knowledge of exponents to simplify each of the following. Write the answers with positive exponents only.

   a) $4^{4} \div 4^{7}$

   b) $3^{-8} \times 3^{5}$

   c) $5^{-4} \times 5^{-2}$

   d) $6^{100} \div 6^{101}$

2.1

2.1E The Zero Exponent

Review the chart at the beginning of Section 2.1D on page 75 of this book. What does 2^0 equal? _____

Review question 1 of the Use Technology and Graphing on page 77 of this book.

What does 2^0 equal? _____

It appears that 2^0 equals _____ .

2.1

Example

Simplify $\dfrac{x^8}{x^8}$.

Method 1: Divide.
You know that anything divided by itself equals _____.

Thus, $\dfrac{x^8}{x^8} = 1$.

Method 2: Use the rule for division of powers.
To divide powers of the same base, subtract the exponents.

Thus, $\dfrac{x^8}{x^8} = x^{8-8}$

$= x^0$

This example used two correct mathematical methods.
This means the two answers must be equivalent.
Thus, $x^0 = 1$, where x is any number except 0.

Write a conclusion about powers with zero exponents.

Practice

1. Use your conclusion and other exponent rules to simplify each of the following:

    a) 3^0

    b) $(2^5)(2^0)$

    c) $(a^2x^5)^0$

    d) $(2^5)(2^3)(2^0)(5^0)$

    e) $(5^{-2})(5^3)(5^0)$

    f) $y^3y^0x^4x^5$

2.1 Completed

Name _____   Date _____

Scientific Notation and Exponents

2.2A Using Scientific Notation

Example 1

24 000 000 × 2 000 000 000	Rewrite each number in scientific notation.
= $(2.4 \times 10^7) \times (2 \times 10^9)$	Rearrange.
= $(2.4 \times 2) \times (10^7 \times 10^9)$	Multiply the numbers, and use exponent rules
= 4.8×10^{16}	to simplify the powers of 10.

Do this problem on your calculator.

What answer appears on your calculator screen? _____

Relate what you see on your calculator screen to your answer above.

Example 2

24 000 000 × 3 000 000	Express each number in scientific notation.
= $(2.4 \times 10^{—}) \times (3 \times 10^{—})$	Rearrange.
= $(2.4 \times 3) \times (10^{—} \times 10^{—})$	Multiply the numbers, and use exponent rules
= $7.2 \times 10^{—}$	to simplify the powers of 10.

Do this problem on your calculator.

What answer appears on your calculator? _____

Relate what you see on your calculator screen to your answer above.

Example 3

24 000 000 ÷ 2 000 000	Rewrite each number in scientific notation.
= $(2.4 \times 10^{—}) \div (2 \times 10^{—})$	Rearrange.
= $(2.4 \div 2) \times (10^7 \div 10^6)$	Divide the numbers, and use exponent rules
= 1.2×10^1	to simplify the powers of 10.

Example 4

24 000 000 ÷ 0.000 002	Rewrite each number in scientific notation.
= $(2.4 \times 10^7) \div (2 \times 10^{-6})$	Rearrange.
= $(\quad \div \quad) \times (10^7 \div 10^{-6})$	Divide the numbers, and use exponent rules
= 1.2×10^{13}	to simplify the powers of 10.

What answer do you expect to see on your calculator? _____

Do this problem on your calculator. Were you right?

Example 5

$24\ 000\ 000\ 000 \div 3000$ Rewrite each number in scientific notation.

$= (2.4 \times 10^{—}) \div (\ \_\_\_\ \times 10^{—})$ Rearrange.

Use your calculator to do this problem.

$= (\qquad\qquad) \times (\qquad\qquad)$ Divide the numbers, and use exponent rules to simplify the powers of 10.

$= _____ \times 10^{—}$

Example 6

$12\ 000\ 000\ 000\ 000 \times 0.000\ 000\ 000\ 3$ Rewrite each number in scientific notation.

$= (_____ \times 10^{—}) \times (3 \times 10^{—})$ Rearrange.

$= (\qquad\qquad) \times (\qquad\qquad)$ Multiply the numbers, and use exponent rules to simplify the powers of 10.

$= _____ \times 10^{—}$

More Exponents and Scientific Notation

Use scientific notation to simplify each of the following.

Example 1

$42\ 000\ 000\ 000\ 000 \times 0.000\ 000\ 000\ 3$

$= (4.2 \times 10^{—}) \times (3 \times 10^{—})$

$= 12.6 \times 10^{—}$ Hint: Rewrite the result in scientific notation.

$= (1.26 \times 10^{1}) \times 10^{—}$

$= 1.26 \times 10^{—}$

Example 2

$42\ 000\ 000\ 000\ 000 \times 0.000\ 000\ 000\ 8$

$= (4.2 \times 10^{—}) \times (8 \times 10^{—})$

$= _____ \times 10^{—}$

$= _____ \times 10^{—}$

$= _____ \times 10^{—}$

2.2

Example 3

42 000 000 000 000 × 72 000 000 000.

(4.2 × 10—) × (_____ × 10—)

_____ × 10—

_____ × 10—

_____ × 10—

Example 4

42 000 000 000 ÷ 0.000 000 000 21

(4.2 × 10—) ÷ (2.1 × 10—)

_____ × 10—

_____ × 10—

Example 5

125 000 000 000 ÷ 0.000 000 000 25

(_____ × 10—) ÷ (_____ × 10—)

_____ × 10—

_____ × 10—

Example 6

42 000 000 000 ÷ 0.000 000 000 84

(4.2 × 10—) ÷ (_____ × 10—)

_____ × 10—

_____ × 10—

Example 7

42 000 000 000 ÷ 0.000 000 126

se your scientific calculator to check your answers.

ook at the picture on this page. Why do you think this picture appears
this section on scientific notation? Discuss with your partner.

2.2 Completed

2.2

Algebra

2.3A Like Terms

In mathematics, you sometimes use **variables** to represent numbers. You often see x, but any letter or symbol will do.

You can then replace the variable in an expression with whatever number is appropriate. This is useful for formulas.

Example 1

The number of people that a fleet of buses will hold is $42x$, where x is the number of buses.

If there are 10 buses, then the number of people the buses can hold is

$42(\quad) = $ _____ .

Example 2

The area of a rectangle is $A = b \times h$, where b represents the base and h represents the height.

If the base of a rectangle is 12 and the height is 10, then the area is

$A = $ _____

When the letter parts of the terms of an expression are exactly the same, then they are **like terms.**

In each line below, circle the terms that are like the first term in the line.

y is a like term to $\qquad$ $3y$ $\quad$ $-y$ $\quad$ xy $\quad$ y^2

x^2 is a like term to $\qquad$ $3x$ $\quad$ $5x^2$ $\quad$ x^3 $\quad$ $2x$

$3x$ is a like term to $\qquad$ $5x$ $\quad$ x^3 $\quad$ $3x^2$ $\quad$ $-4x$

You can add and subtract like terms by adding and subtracting the coefficient in front of each variable. For example, $2x + 10x = 12x$.

Practice

. Simplify each expression by adding the like terms.

a) $5x + 7x$

b) $2x^2 - 3x + 3x^2 + 5x$

= _____

= _____

c) $y + 2 + y + 3$

d) $3y^2 + 2y + 4 + y^2 + y + 1$

e) $x^2 + 2 - x^2 + 3x + 1$

f) $3y^2 + 4y + 2 - y^2 + y - 2$

. Write 3 terms that are like the term x^2.

. Write 3 terms that are like the term $4xy$.

. Underline the terms that are like $5x$.

$3x$	$-2x$	$5x^2$	x^5	$2xy$
5	$5y$	$-5x$	$-2000x$	$-(3)(-5)x$

Explain why x^2 and $2x$ are not like terms.

2.3

2.3B How to Handle Brackets

When you have to simplify an expression like $3x(x + 2)$, the brackets mean that you are to multiply the expression outside the bracket by each term inside the bracket. This is the **distributive property.**

Remove the brackets from the expression in each example. The first one is done for you.

2.3

Example 1

$2(x + 4)$ (2 times x, then, 2 times 4)
$= 2x + 8$

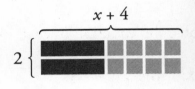

Example 2

$2(3x + 5)$

$=$

Example 3

$-3(2x + 4)$

$=$

Example 4

$2x(3x - 4)$ Remember your exponent rules.

$=$

Example 5

$5(x + 4) + 2(4x + 1)$ Simplify the answer by collecting like terms.

$=$

$=$

Example 6

$2x(3x + 4) - 4(x + 4)$

$=$

$=$

Example 7

$-3x(2x - 4) - (x^2 + 3x + 5)$

$=$

$=$

2.3C Solving Equations

Your goal in solving equations is to find the value of the unknown that makes the equation true.

There is one rule. Isolate the unknown by performing the same mathematical operation to each side of the equation (like balancing a scale), until the term with the unknown is by itself on one side of the equal sign and a number is on the other side.

Solve the equation in each of the following examples.

Example 1

$x + 5 = 12$ Subtract 5 from each side.

$-5 \quad -5$

$x = 7$ Check by substituting into the original equation.

Example 2

$x - 7 = 8$ Add 7 to each side.

$x = 15$

Example 3

$x - 5 = 7$ Add 5 to each side.

Divide both sides by 3.

Example 4

$(x - 5) = 6$ Remove the brackets first.

2.3

Name ______________________ Date ______________

Example 5

$4x + 8 = 2x + 4$

Collect the terms in x on one side of the equation. Thus, subtract $2x$ from each side.

2.3

Example 6

$5x - 5 = 6x + 8$

Check the answer by substituting $x =$ ______

L.S.	R.S.

Example 7

$3(x - 5) = 2(2x + 1)$

Check the answer by substituting $x =$ ______

L.S.	R.S.

Example 8

$5x - 4 + 4x = 7 + 2x + 3$

Check the answer by substituting $x =$ ______

L.S.	R.S.

2.3D Magic Equations: Magic Square

Solve each of the following equations in the chart. If your answers are correct, you will get the same sum every time you add up a column, a row, or a diagonal. Check that this is so.

$2x + 8 = 24$	$4y - 2y = 58$	$10 + 2x = 70$	$7x = 2x + 10$
$2x - 5 = 31$	$2x + 10 = 38$	$7x = 5x + 26$	$5y - 10 = 110$
$2a - 10 = 12$	$n + 5 = 27$	$2(x - 3) = 34$	$2x - 3 = 29$
$4(x - 2) = 120$	$7m + 3 = 5m + 11$	$x^2 = 36, x > 0$	$11x - 4 = 9x + 50$

What is the **magic sum** of the magic square? _____

2.3E Algebra: Practice

2.3

1. Simplify.

   a) $3x - 4 + 5x + 9$

   b) $-3y + 4x - 5y - 6x$

   c) $3m + 9m - 2m + 9k$

   d) $5x^2 - 6s - 7x^2 + 9s$

   e) $3(2m + 2) - 2(4 - m)$

   f) $3(3z - 2) + 3(2z + 5)$

2. Evaluate your answer in question 1 b) if $x = 3$ and $y = -2$.

3. Solve each equation. Check your answers. Show your work.

   a) $2x - 4 = 22$

   b) $4m + 11 = m + 17$

   c) $3x - 12 = 4x + 3$

   d) $3m - 2 + 2m = 13$

   e) $2(x - 7) = 4(3x + 1)$

   Check question 3 b).

L.S.	R.S.

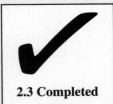

2.3 Completed

Slopes

2.4A Slopes of Staircases and Ramps

. For each staircase, count squares to determine the rise and the run and
calculate the **slope.** Remember, slope = $\frac{\text{rise}}{\text{run}}$.

a)

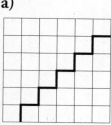

b)

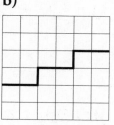

c)

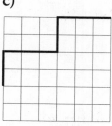

d)

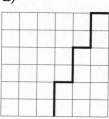

2.4

Rise =   Rise =   Rise =   Rise =

Run =   Run =   Run =   Run =

Slope =   Slope =   Slope =   Slope =

. For each ramp, measure the rise and the run in millimetres, and
calculate the slope. Put a star * beside the steepest ramp.

a)   b)   c)   d)

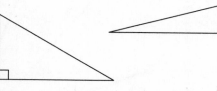

Rise =   Rise =   Rise =   Rise =

Run =   Run =   Run =   Run =

Slope =   Slope =   Slope =   Slope =

3. For each line, count squares to determine the rise and the run, and calculate the slope.

a)   b)   c)   d)

 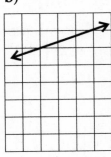  

Rise =   Rise =   Rise =   Rise =

Run =   Run =   Run =   Run =

Slope =   Slope =   Slope =   Slope =

4. If a line slants upward from left to right, it has a positive slope.
If a line slants downward from left to right, it has a negative slope.

lines with positive slope   lines with negative slope

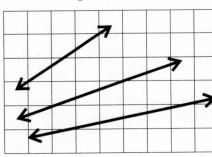 

How do the slopes of the lines relate to the correlations studied in Unit 1?

. Find the slope of each of the following lines.
(Be careful of negative slopes!!)

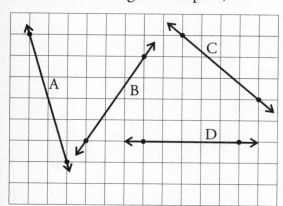

A: Rise =   B: Rise =   C: Rise =   D: Rise =

Run =   Run =   Run =   Run =

Slope =   Slope =   Slope =   Slope =

Find the slope of each line. Note that each unit on the scale may not
be 1.

a)

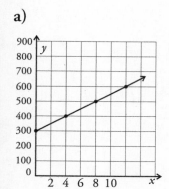

b)

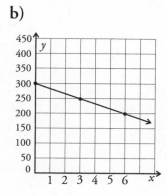

c)

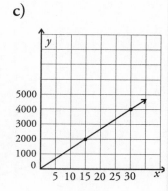

Rise =   Rise =   Rise =

Run =   Run =   Run =

Slope =   Slope =   Slope =

7. The steeper the line the _____ the slope.

2.4B Finding Slopes of Stairs

Pair–Share   Student A does part a) of a question.
Student B coaches Student A.
The roles are reversed for part b) of the question.

1. Find the slope of each staircase by counting squares.

   a)

   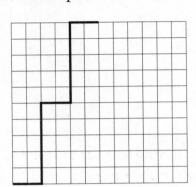

   b)

   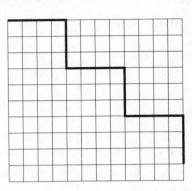

2. Find the slope of each line by counting squares.

   a)

   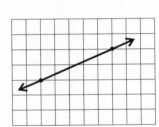

   b)

3. Find the slope of each ramp.

   a)

   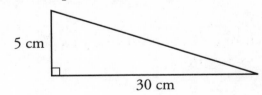

   b)

   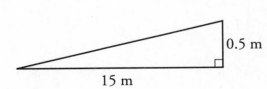

. Find the slope of this line in two different ways.

a) Student A's way

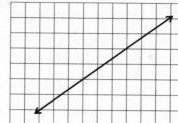

b) Student B's way

c) Discuss why the answers of all of the students should be the same. Can you think of a third way to find the slope?

. Draw a line segment with the given slope.

a) slope $\dfrac{5}{7}$

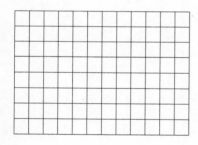

b) slope $-\dfrac{5}{7}$

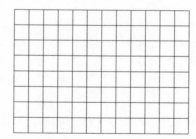

. Working together, match each line to the most likely slope. Discuss why you think these are the correct slopes.

slopes: 3 __ 5 __ $\dfrac{1}{3}$ __ $-\dfrac{1}{5}$ __ 1 __ -3 __ 0 __

lines:

A   B   C   D   E   F   G

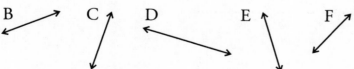

2.4

2.4C Finding Slopes of Ramps

Part A
With a classmate, find a ramp, either in the school or in town. Do not forget to take a tape measure or a metre stick and writing equipment.

Measure the height (rise) _____ and the

length (run) _____ of your ramp.

Part B
Make a scale drawing of your ramp.

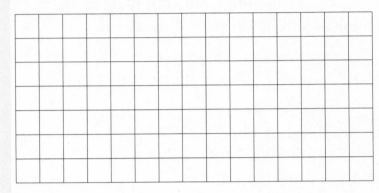

Scale:
1 side length of
each square =

_____

Part C
Determine the slope of the ramp.

Part D
The health and safety inspector says,
"The rise to run of a ramp must not be greater than 1 to 12."

In other words, the slope cannot be greater than $\frac{1}{12}$.

Does your ramp pass the safety test? _____
Explain:

2.4D Assignment: Slopes of Stairs and Ramps

1. Find a staircase at home or at school.

   a) Where is it? _____

   b) How many steps does it have? _____

2. Measure the rise and the run of a step of your staircase.

   rise _____   run _____

3. Find the slope of the staircase.

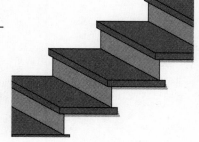

2.4

4. Choose a scale and make a scale drawing of the staircase.

   Scale: 1 side length of each square = _____

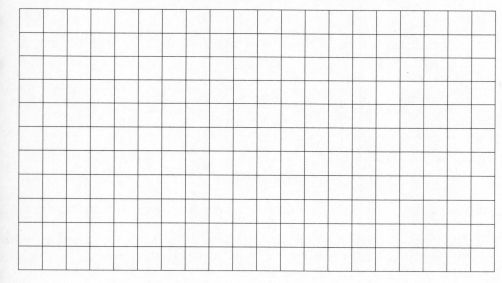

5. Would these stairs be safe for children who could use stairs with a slope no greater than $\dfrac{2}{3}$? Show your work and explain your answer.

6. Find a ramp at your home or at school.

Where is it? _____

7. Measure the rise and the run of the ramp.

rise _____   run _____

8. Find the slope of the ramp.

2.4

9. Make a scale drawing of the ramp.

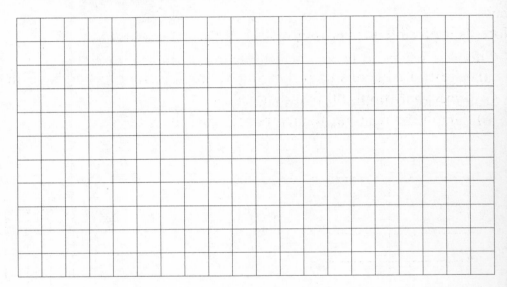

10. Would this ramp be safe for wheelchair users who should use a ramp with a slope no greater than $\dfrac{1}{12}$? Show your work and explain your answer.

2.4 Completed

Linear Models

2.5A Modelling Linear Relationships

Problem 1

Rachel works at a fitness centre and receives a base pay of $20 per day, plus a bonus of $5.00 for each trial pass she gives away. This can be modelled by the equation

$$P = 5s + 20$$

where P represents her total pay for a day and s represents the number of trial passes she gives away.

(Note: Is it possible for her to give away a part of a trial pass?)

a) Create a table of values showing her total earnings for a day if she gives away up to 30 free trial passes.

b) Graph the relation. Remember to label the axes.

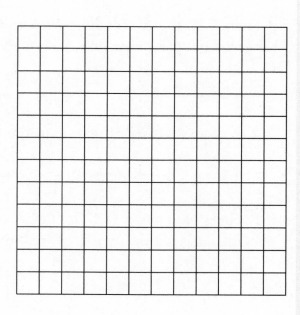

2. **a)** Identify the slope of the line and the *P*-intercept of the line.

    b) How do these relate to Rachel's total pay?
(Show any necessary work.)

    Slope   How it relates.

    P-intercept   How it relates.

2.5

3. **a)** One day, Rachel was paid a total of $45 (base pay plus bonus). Use your graph to find how many trial passes she gave away that day.

    _____

    b) Another day, Rachel gave away 4 trial passes. Use your equation to find her total pay, including bonus, for that day.

    _____

4. If Rachel's base pay remains $20 per day, but her bonus amount is $6 for each trial pass, how does the graph change?

    _____

    In this case, what equation would represent her total pay?

    _____

5. If Rachel's base pay was $25, but her bonus amount for each trial pass remained at $5, how would the graph change?

    _____

    In this case, what equation would represent her total daily pay (base pay plus bonus)?

    _____

Part B

Problem

The total cost, C, of repairing a furnace is $40 per visit plus $35/h. This cost can be modelled by the equation

$C =$ _____$h +$ _____ , where h is the length of time in hours.

Note: Time can be charged in fractions of an hour.)

2.5

. **a)** Create a table of values showing the total charges for a visit that could last up to 10 h.
   b) Graph the relation.

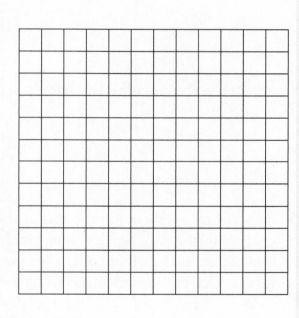

. Identify the slope and the C-intercept of your line.
How do these relate to the total cost?
(Show any necessary work.)

Slope   How it relates.

C-intercept   How it relates.

3. a) Use your graph to find the length of the visit, if your total cost was $145.

_____

b) Use your equation to find the total cost, if the length of the visit was 5.5 h.

_____

2.5

4. a) If the initial charge stayed the same, but the rate changed to $40.00/h, how would the graph change?

b) Write the equation that would represent the new cost.

5. Another company made a graph to show its charges for furnace repairs. This graph lay at the same angle as the other company's graph, but its initial price per visit changed to $50.

a) Describe what this means in terms of their charges for repairs.

b) Write the equation that models the new charges for repairs.

2.5B   Modelling Linear Relationships: Pair–Share

Pair–Share: Partner A completes Problem A.
                    Partner B coaches Partner A.

Problem A

The cost, C, of a cell phone with the You Call Company is $20 per month for the phone, plus $0.50 per additional minute. This cost can be modelled by the equation

$$C = 0.50t + 20,$$

where t is the number of additional minutes.
(Note: Time can be charged in fractions of a minute.)

2.5

.   a) Create a table of values showing the total charges for a month for up to 15 additional minutes.
    b) Graph the relation.

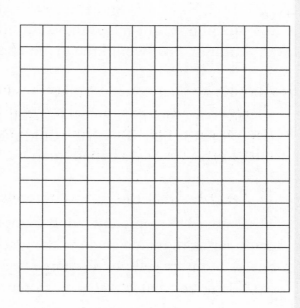

2. Identify the slope and the *C*-intercept of your line.
   How do these relate to the total charges?
   (Show any necessary work.)
   Slope   How it relates.

   C-intercept   How it relates.

3. If your monthly charges are $24, for how many additional
   minutes did you use the phone?

4. a) If the You Call Company continued to charge $20 per month for
       the phone, but raised the additional time rate to $0.75 per
       minute, how would the graph change?

    b) Write the equation that would model the new cost after the
       changes.

5. The Listen Up Company made a graph of its cell phone charges. This
   graph lay at the same angle as the graph of the You Call Company,
   but its monthly cell phone charge was $30.
   a) Describe what this means, in terms of the cost of the phone with
      the Listen Up Company.

   b) Write the equation that models the cost of a phone with the
      Listen Up Company.

Name _____   Date _____

Pair–Share: Partner B completes Problem B.

Partner A coaches Partner B.

Problem B

The total cost, *C*, of repairs with the Fixit Company is $60 per visit, plus $30/h. This cost can be modelled by the equation

$$C = \underline{\hspace{1cm}} h + \underline{\hspace{1cm}} \text{, where } h \text{ is the length of time in hours.}$$

(Note: Time can be charged in fractions of an hour.)

. **a)** Create a table of values showing the total cost for a visit that could last up to 10 h.

b) Graph the relation.

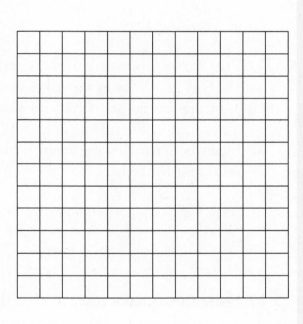

. Identify the slope and the *C*-intercept of your line.
How do these relate to the total cost?
(Show any necessary work.)

Slope   How it relates.

C-intercept   How it relates.

3. If your total cost is $105, for how many hours was the visit?

2.5

4. a) If the initial charge stayed the same, but the hourly rate changed to $40.00, how would the graph change?

b) Write the equation that would represent the new total cost.

5. The PipeWorks Company made a graph to show its charges for repairs. This graph lay at the same angle as The Fixit Company's graph, but its initial price per visit was $50.

a) Describe what this means in terms of The PipeWorks Company's total cost for repairs.

b) Write the equation that models the new total cost for repairs.

2.5 Completed

The Cartesian Plane

The *xy*-plane is also called the _____ plane and is named after the mathematician

_____ _____.

The horizontal axis is called the ___ -axis, and the _____ axis is called the *y*-axis.

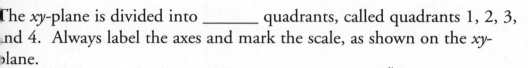

They meet at the _____.

All points can be labelled with _____ and expressed as ordered pairs, (,   ).

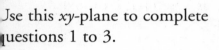

The *xy*-plane is divided into _____ quadrants, called quadrants 1, 2, 3, and 4. Always label the axes and mark the scale, as shown on the *xy*-plane.

2.6

Use this *xy*-plane to complete questions 1 to 3.

1. State the coordinates of each point.

H_____, K_____,

M_____, P_____,

Q_____, R_____

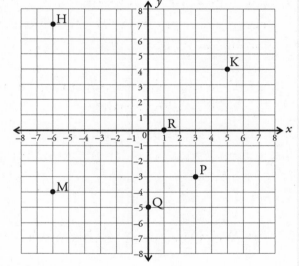

2. Graph these points. Include the labels.

A(2, 3), B(5, −1), C(−2, 3), D(−4, −5), E(0, 3), F(−4, 0)

3. **a)** Plot 3 points, with each point in a different quadrant.
   b) Trade books with a classmate.
   Find the coordinates of the points plotted by your classmate.
   c) Exchange books, and check if you agree with the answer.

2.6 Completed

The Equation $y = mx + b$

2.7A Linear Equations $y = mx + b$ Using Graphing Technology

Use your graphing calculator or computer to complete each exercise.

Exercise 1: Linear Equations

Using a Graphing Calculator
1. Set the window values.
2. Input $Y_1 = 2x + 3$
$Y_2 = 3x$
$Y_3 = -4x - 1$
Press **GRAPH**.

Using Graphmatica
Input $y = 2x + 3$
$y = 3x$
$y = -4x - 1$
Press **GRAPH**

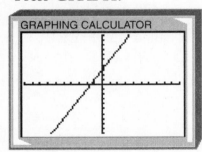

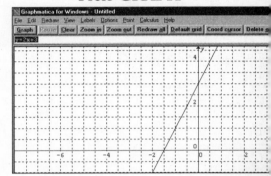

All the graphs are _____

Exercise 2: Non-Linear Equations

Use a new screen for each question. To enter x^2 press **x**, **^**, and then, **2**.

Using a Graphing Calculator
1. Set the window values.

2. Input $Y_1 = x^2$
$Y_2 = x^3 - 2$
$Y_3 = \dfrac{1}{x}$
Press **GRAPH**.

Using Graphmatica
Input $y = x^2$

$y = x^3 - 2$

$y = \dfrac{1}{x}$

Press **GRAPH**

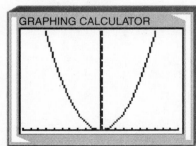

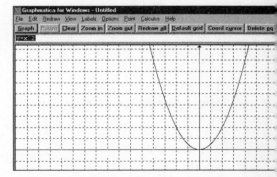

All the graphs are _____

Name _____   Date _____

Underline the equations of straight lines. Use your graphing calculator or computer to check your answers.

a) $y = 2x - 1$ **b)** $y = x^2 + 2$ **c)** $x = y^2$

d) $x - y = 1$ **e)** $x = y^3$ **f)** $x = y + 5$

Exercise 3: Parallel Lines and Intercepts
Use a new screen for each question.

1. **a)** Graph the following lines on the same set of axes.
   b) What is the slope of each line?
   c) What are the coordinates of the point at which each line crosses the y-axis?

Equation	Slope	y-intercept
A: $y = 2x + 5$		
B: $y = 2x - 8$		
C: $y = 2x + 3$		

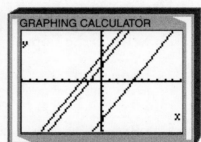

GRAPHING CALCULATOR

d) Study your the chart.
   How are the three lines the same?

   How do the three lines differ?

2. Guess what the graph of $y = 2x - 4$ will look like. Complete the blanks.

a) The coordinates of the point at which this line will cross

   the y-axis are _____ .

   The slope of this line will be _____ .

b) Use your graphing calculator or computer to check your guess.

Were you right? _____

3. **a)** Guess the equation of the line that crosses the y-axis at 1 and has a slope of 2.

_____

b) Use your graphing calculator or computer to check.

Were you right? _____

4. **a)** Use your graphing calculator or computer to graph the lines. Use the same screen for all of the graphs.
    b) What are the coordinates of the point at which the line crosses the y-axis?
    c) What is the slope?

Equation	Slope	y-intercept
A: $y = -3x + 2$		
B: $y = -3x - 4$		
C: $y = -3x$		

d) Study your chart.
How are the three lines the same?

How do the three lines differ?

5. a) Guess what the graph of $y = -3x + 5$ will look like.
The coordinates of the point at which this line will cross the

y-axis are _____ .

The slope of this line will be _____ .

b) Use your graphing calculator or computer to check your guess.

Were you right? _____

2.7

6. a) Guess the equation of a line that has a y-intercept of 5 and a

slope of –3. _____.

b) Use your graphing calculator or computer to check your guess.

Were you right? _____

7. Write some conclusions from your work in questions 5 and 6 by
finishing the following statements:

a) Given $y = \square x + \triangle$, $\square$ is the coefficient of x and tells you the

_____

$\triangle$ is the constant term and tells you the

_____

b) In general, the equation of a line is $y = mx + b$, where _____
represents the slope and _____ represents the y-intercept.

c) Lines that are parallel have the _____ _____ .

d) Use your conclusions to help you write the equation of each line.

(i) slope of 4 and y-intercept of 3 _____

(ii) slope of –2 and y-intercept of 7 _____

(iii) $m = \dfrac{1}{2}$ and $b = -3$ _____

8. Using your conclusions, state the slope and y-intercept of each of the following. Use your graphing calculator or computer to check your answers.

   a) $y = -3x - 4$; slope = _____, y-intercept = _____
      Does it check?

   b) $y = \dfrac{3}{5}x - 2$; slope = _____, y-intercept = _____
      Does it check?

   c) $y = -\dfrac{1}{2}x + 4$; m = _____, b = _____
      Does it check?

Exercise 4: Perpendicular Lines
Use a new screen for each question.

1. On the same set of axes, graph

   $y = 2x - 7$ and $y = -\dfrac{1}{2}x + 2$.

   What appears to be true about the angle made by these lines?

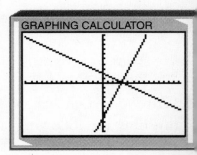

GRAPHING CALCULATOR

_____

2. On the same set of axes, graph $y = -10x - 5$ and $y = \dfrac{1}{10}x - 2$.

   What appears to be true about the angle made by these lines?

_____

3. On the same set of axes, graph $y = -\dfrac{1}{4}x + 3$ and $y = 4x + 2$.

   What appears to be true about the angle made by these lines?

_____

4. On the same set of axes, graph $y = \dfrac{2}{3}x + 5$ and $y = -x + 1$.

   What appears to be true about the angle made by these lines?

_____

2.7

. For each pair of equations in questions 1 to 4, notice the coefficient of
x. (This coefficient is m that represents the slope.)
Make some conclusions by filling in the blanks in these statements:

a) If the slopes of two lines are negative reciprocals, then the

lines are _____.

b) If lines are perpendicular, then their slopes are

_____   _____.

. State the slope (m) for the given equation. Then, state the slope of a
line that is perpendicular to it. ($\perp$ means *is perpendicular to*.)

a) $y = 3x - 4$

b) $y = -\dfrac{1}{2}x + 5$

c) $y = \dfrac{17}{11}x - 3$

$m =$

$m =$

$m =$

$m\perp =$

$m\perp =$

$m\perp =$

Exercise 5: Family of Lines, Same y-intercept

. Graph on the same set of axes.

$y = x$ $y = 3x$ $y = -2x$ $y = -\dfrac{1}{4}x$

What is the y-intercept of each line? _____
The only way in which the lines are different is

_____

These lines have a common characteristic; they have the same
y-intercept. In this question, it is zero. This is called a **family of lines**.

How many more lines can you write that are in this family?

_____

2. Write the equations of 3 other lines in this family.

    A: _____   **B:** _____   **C:** _____

3. On the same screen, graph three lines that belong to the family $y = mx - 2$. Write down the equations that you have chosen.

    A: _____   **B:** _____   **C:** _____

The y-intercept that this family of lines shares is _____.

Each member of the family has a different _____.

4. Circle the lines that belong to the same family as $y = 4x - 7$.

    $y = 3x - 7$ $y = 3x + 7$ $y = 2x$ $y = -4x - 7$

Exercise 6: More Families, Same Slope

1. Another family of lines will have the same slope.
For example, $y = 3x + b$ represents the family with slope 3.
Graph four lines in the family $y = 3x + b$.
Write down the equations that you have chosen.

    A: _____   **B:** _____

    C: _____   **D:** _____

Should all of your lines be parallel? Explain.

Did the *y*-intercept change each time? Explain.

2. Describe the graphs of the lines in the family $y = -2x + b$.

Name 3 lines that would be in this family. Check your results.

A: _____   B: _____   C: _____

3. Circle the lines in the same family as $y = 4x - 7$.

$y = 3x + 7$ $y = 4x - 1$ $y = 4x$ $y = -4x - 1$

Exercise 7: Horizontal and Vertical Lines

. Discuss with a classmate what you think the graph of $y = 4$ will look like.

a) Graph $y = 4$. Describe this line.

b) Graph $y = -2$. Describe this line.

c) Graph $y = 0$. Describe this line.

d) Guess what $y = -5$ will look like. Check your guess.

e) Write a conclusion by filling in the blanks.
   Conclusion
   The equations of all horizontal lines are of the form

   _____.

   The slope of a horizontal line is _____

2. With a classmate, decide what you think the graph of $x = 4$ will look like.

a) Graph $x = 4$. Describe this line.

b) Graph $x = -2$. Describe this line.

c) Graph $x = 0$. Describe this line.

d) Guess what $x = -5$ will look like. Check your guess.

e) Write a conclusion by filling in the blanks.
   Conclusion
   The equations of all vertical lines are of the form

   _____.

   The slope of a vertical line is _____

3. Circle the equations of lines that are horizontal, and underline the equations of lines that are vertical.

   a) $y = 4$ b) $x = 3$ c) $y = x - 1$

   d) $x = 3$ e) $x = y - 3$ f) $x + y = 1$

   g) $y = 700$ h) $x = -20$ i) $y = x$

2.7B Lines and More Lines

Use the conclusions from the computer investigation on pages 106 to 114 of this book.

1. The equation of any line can be written as $y =$ _____ $x +$ _____ .

2. You write $y = mx + b$, where m is the _____ and

   b is the _____ .

	Equation	Slope	y-intercept
a)	$y = 2x + 3$		
b)	$y = -2x + 1$		
c)	$y = \dfrac{1}{2} x + 4$		
d)	$y = -3x - 2$		

3. You can use the slope and y-intercept as a shortcut to graphing the lines.
   - First, place a dot on the y-intercept.
   - Starting at the y-intercept, use the slope to find a second point.
   - Join these points carefully with a ruler.

   Use this method to graph lines in parts a), b), c), and d) in the table above. Label your lines.

4. You can find the equation of a line if you can read its slope and y-intercept from the graph.
   - Find the y-intercept. (This is b.)
   - Find the coordinates of another point on the line. Find the slope. (This is m.)
   - Write the equation of each line by substituting the values of m and b in $y = mx + b$.

   Use this method to find the equation of each line shown below.

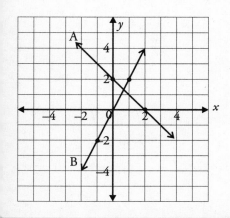
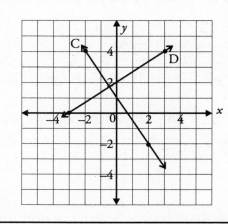

A: _____

B: _____

C: _____

D: _____

5. Parallel lines are lines that _____.

Slopes of parallel lines are _____.

a) All lines that are parallel to $y = 2x + 5$ have a slope of ____.

b) Write the equation of 3 lines that are parallel to the line in a).

_____   _____   _____

c) All lines that are parallel to $y = -\frac{4}{5}x + 1$ have a slope of ____.

d) Write the equations of 3 lines that are parallel to the line in c).

_____   _____   _____

6. Perpendicular lines are lines that _____.

Slopes of perpendicular lines are _____ _____.

a) All lines that are perpendicular to $y = 2x + 5$ have a slope of ____.

b) Write the equations of 3 lines that are perpendicular to this line.

_____   _____   _____

c) All lines that are perpendicular to $y = -\frac{3}{2}x - 4$ have a slope

of ____.

d) Write the equation of 3 lines that are perpendicular to this line.

_____   _____   _____

e) All lines that are perpendicular to $y = -\frac{1}{4}x + 2$ have a slope of ____

f) Write the equations of 3 lines that are perpendicular to this line.

_____   _____   _____

2.7C Equations of Lines: Chart

1. Complete the chart.

Equation	Slope	y-intercept	Slope of Line Parallel to This Line	Slope of Line Perpendicular to This Line
1. $y = 5x + 1$				
2. $y = -2x - 7$				
3. $y = \dfrac{3}{5}x + 2$				
4.	2	7		
5.		8	-4	
6.		3		$\dfrac{1}{4}$
7.		5		-2
8.		0	$\dfrac{2}{3}$	
9. $y = x$				
10. $y = 7$				
11. $x = 2$				

2. Write the equation of each line segment in the diagram below.

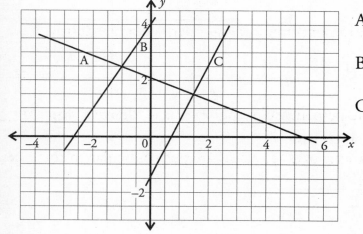

A: _____

B: _____

C: _____

2.7D Find the Equation of a Line

The equation of a line is $y = mx + b$, where m is the slope and b is the y-intercept.

For each of the following pairs of points,
a) use the grid to plot the points
b) draw a line through the points. Extend the line, if necessary.
c) find the slope, m, and the y-intercept, b, of the line
d) write the equation of the line

2.7

1. A(1, 2), B(–2, –1)

    $m =$ _____, $b =$ _____
    Equation of line AB is

    _____

2. C(2, 4), D(–2, –2)

    $m =$ _____, $b =$ _____
    Equation of line CD is

    _____

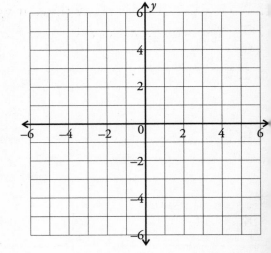

3. E(4, 2), F(–2, 5)

    $m =$ _____, $b =$ _____
    Equation of line EF is

    _____

4. G(1, 2), H(2, –1)

    $m =$ _____, $b =$ _____
    Equation of line GH is

    _____

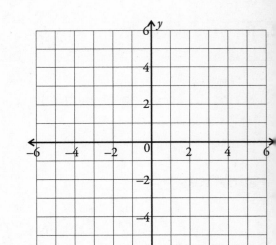

2.7E Find the Equation of the Line That Represents the Cost

For each of the following,

a) use the given information to write the coordinates (number, cost)
   for two points
b) insert an appropriate scale on the grid and plot the two sets of
   coordinates you wrote
c) draw a line through the points and extend the line to the vertical axis
d) find the rate (slope, *m*) and the initial cost (*y*-intercept, *b*)
e) write the equation of the line that represents the total cost

2.7

1. To have your lawn cut 5 times it would cost you $350. (,   )
   To have your lawn cut 8 times it would cost you $500. (,   )

rate _____

initial cost _____

equation of line

_____

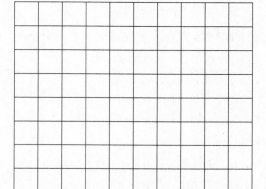

2. It costs $450 to hold a party for 50 people. (,   )
   It costs $300 to hold a party for 30 people. (,   )

rate _____

initial cost _____

equation of line

_____

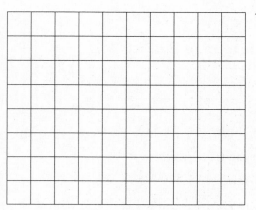

3. a) A ride in a cab costs $6.50 for 3 km. (,   )
A ride in a cab costs $11 for 6 km. (,   )

rate _____

initial cost _____

equation of line

_____

b) Use your equation and your graph to find the cost of an 8-km taxi ride in this taxi.

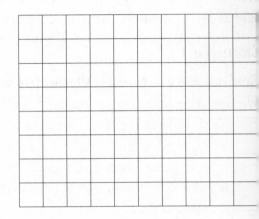

4. a) It costs $110 to print 30 books. (,   )
It costs $230 to print 90 books. (,   )

rate _____

initial cost _____

equation of line

_____

b) Use your equation and your graph to find the cost to print 60 books.

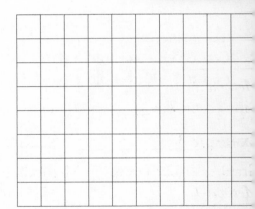

2.7F Graphing Lines: Three Methods

To graph a straight line you need at least _____ points.
Method 1 Use a table of values. *Method 2* Use the *y*-intercept and slope.
Method 3 Use the *x*- and *y*-intercepts.

Example 1

Graph $y = 3x - 2$ using Methods 1 and 2.
Method 1

x	y

Method 2
-intercept, $b =$ _____   slope, $m =$ _____

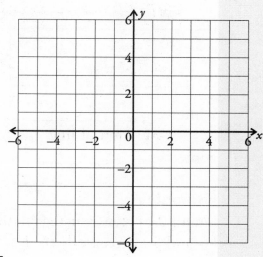

Example 2

Graph $y = \frac{1}{2} x + 5$ using Methods 1 and 2.
Method 1

x	y

Method 2
-intercept, $b =$ _____   slope, $m =$ _____

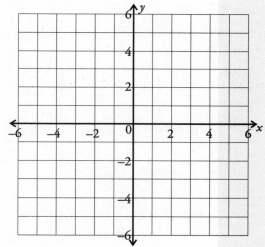

Example 3

Graph $y = -2x + 3$ using Methods 1 and 2.
Method 1

x	y

Method 2
-intercept, $b =$ _____   slope, $m =$ _____

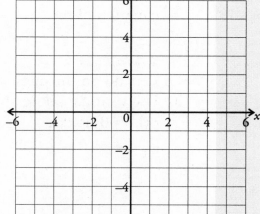

Example 4

Graph $2x - 3y = 6$ using Method 3
(x- and y-intercepts).

x	y
0	
	0

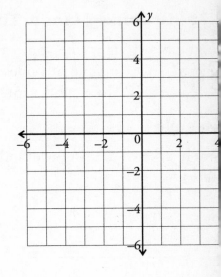

x-intercept _____

y-intercept _____

Example 5

Graph $2x + 4y = 4$ using Method 3
(x- and y-intercepts).

x	y
0	
	0

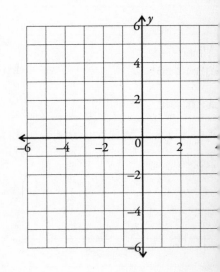

x-intercept _____

y-intercept _____

Discuss which method you find easiest and why.

Does it depend on the question? Explain.

2.7 Completed

Linear Models for Comparison Shopping

2.8A Example of Comparison Shopping

You decided to join an indoor tennis club for the winter. The club had 3 different plans.

You estimated the number of hours of tennis you would likely play in a year in order to decide which was the best plan for you for one year.

Plan A: membership fee of $200, plus $15.00/h court time
Plan B: membership fee of $250, plus $10.00/h court time
Plan C: no membership fee, $25.00/h court time

a) Find the equation to represent the cost of each plan.

Plan A Equation _____

Plan B Equation _____

Plan C Equation _____

b) Draw a graph of each plan. Use 30 hours as the number of hours of play in the year.

Plan A

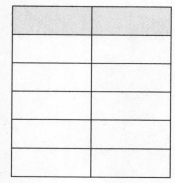

Plan B

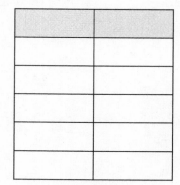

Plan C

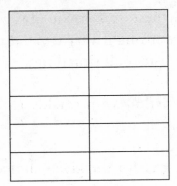

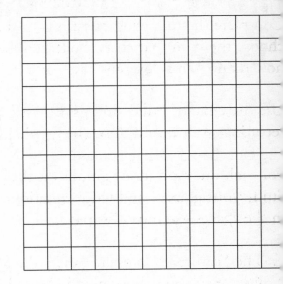

c) Decide which is the best buy for different numbers of hours.

Conclusion

I would choose Plan A if I were planning to play between

_____ and _____ hours of tennis.

I would choose Plan B if I were planning to play between

_____ and _____ hours of tennis.

I would choose Plan C if I were planning to play between

_____ and _____ hours of tennis.

Name _____   Date _____

2.8B Comparison Shopping: Practice

Complete the following questions to find the best deal, if you always choose the item that costs the least. The answer might vary depending on how many items you purchase. Be sure to consider all situations.

Use the table of values and grid master provided by your teacher to record the values and draw the graphs.

For each question, draw graphs on the same grid for the given choices. Study your graphs, and write equations that represent the given choices in the spaces given on this page.

1. The Yearbook Company offers the following prices.
   Price A: $100 set-up, plus $15 per book
   Price B: $300 set-up, plus $10 per book
   You want to print no more than 200 books.

Equation for price A _____

Equation for price B _____

Which is the better price?

2. The T-Shirt Company offers the following prices.
   Price A: $20 for set-up, plus $5 per shirt
   Price B: $15 for set-up, plus $8 per shirt
   These prices are for a maximum of 10 T-shirts.

Equation for price A _____

Equation for price B _____

Which is the better price?

3. Three window cleaning companies offer the following prices.
Price A: $30 for supplies, plus $4 per window
Price B: $7 per window
You have 15 windows to clean.

Equation for price A _____

Equation for price B _____

Which is the better price?

2.8

4. Three book binding companies offer the following prices.
Price A: $150 for shipping, plus $4.50 per book.
Price B: $300 for shipping, plus $3.00 per book.
Price C: $8.00 per book
You want to have a maximum of 100 books bound.

Equation for price A _____

Equation for price B _____

Equation for price C _____

Which is the best price?

5. The price for decorator A is $200 for the first visit, plus $20/h.
The price for decorator B is $300 for the first visit, plus $20/h.
The price for decorator C is $200 for the first visit, plus $25/h.

Equation for price A _____

Equation for price B _____

Equation for price C _____

Which is the best price?

2.8 Completed

These awards are to help you keep track of your successes in the grade 9
applied course. Your teacher will instruct you as to how you will use
them. Keep up the good work.

Congratulations

2.1 Completed on
_____

Signatures _____

_____

Comments:

Achievement:
Thinking/Inquiry: 1, 2, 3, 4, NA
Communication: 1, 2, 3, 4, NA
Knowledge: 1, 2, 3, 4, NA
Application: 1, 2, 3, 4, NA

Congratulations

2.2 Completed on
_____

Signatures _____

_____

Comments:

Achievement:
Thinking/Inquiry: 1, 2, 3, 4, NA
Communication: 1, 2, 3, 4, NA
Knowledge: 1, 2, 3, 4, NA
Application: 1, 2, 3, 4, NA

UNIT 2

Congratulations

2.3 Completed on
_____

Signatures _____

_____

Comments:

Achievement:
Thinking/Inquiry: 1, 2, 3, 4, NA
Communication: 1, 2, 3, 4, NA
Knowledge: 1, 2, 3, 4, NA
Application: 1, 2, 3, 4, NA

Congratulations

2.4 Completed on
_____

Signatures _____

_____

Comments:

Achievement:
Thinking/Inquiry: 1, 2, 3, 4, NA
Communication: 1, 2, 3, 4, NA
Knowledge: 1, 2, 3, 4, NA
Application: 1, 2, 3, 4, NA

Congratulations

2.5 Completed on

_____

Signatures_____

_____

Comments:

Achievement:
Thinking/Inquiry: 1, 2, 3, 4, NA
Communication: 1, 2, 3, 4, NA
Knowledge: 1, 2, 3, 4, NA
Application: 1, 2, 3, 4, NA

Congratulations

2.6 Completed on

_____

Signatures_____

_____

Comments:

Achievement:
Thinking/Inquiry: 1, 2, 3, 4, NA
Communication: 1, 2, 3, 4, NA
Knowledge: 1, 2, 3, 4, NA
Application: 1, 2, 3, 4, NA

Congratulations

2.7 Completed on

_____

Signatures_____

_____

Comments:

Achievement:
Thinking/Inquiry: 1, 2, 3, 4, NA
Communication: 1, 2, 3, 4, NA
Knowledge: 1, 2, 3, 4, NA
Application: 1, 2, 3, 4, NA

Congratulations

2.8 Completed on

_____

Signatures_____

_____

Comments:

Achievement:
Thinking/Inquiry: 1, 2, 3, 4, NA
Communication: 1, 2, 3, 4, NA
Knowledge: 1, 2, 3, 4, NA
Application: 1, 2, 3, 4, NA

UNIT 2

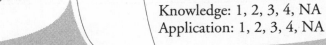

3 Relationships in Geometry

Area and Perimeter

3.1A Rectangles

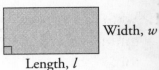

Width, w

Area of a rectangle, $A =$ _____ × _____

Length, l

Perimeter of a rectangle, $P =$ _____ + _____

$$= 2 (\underline{\hspace{1.5cm}} + \underline{\hspace{1.5cm}})$$

1. Find the area, A, and the perimeter, P, of each shape.

   a)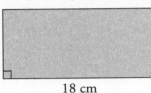

   12 cm

   18 cm

   $A =$ _____ × _____

   $=$

   $P = 2(\underline{\hspace{1cm}} + \underline{\hspace{1cm}})$

   $=$

   $=$

   b)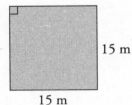

   15 m

   15 m

   $A =$

   $P =$

   c)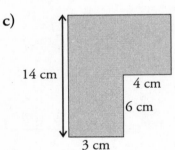

   14 cm

   4 cm

   6 cm

   3 cm

   $A = A_{(\text{rectangle 1})} + A_{(\text{rectangle 2})}$

   The perimeter is the total distance around.

   $P =$

2. Draw and label a diagram of a rectangle.
   Exchange your diagram with that of a classmate.
   Find the area and the perimeter of your classmate's diagram.
   Check each other's work.

3.1

3.1B Area and Perimeter: Class Activity

1. With a partner, choose a rectangular shape in the room, such as the chalkboard, a door, or a desk top.

State your choice:_____

2. **a)** Measure your shape, using appropriate units.

   Length: _____ Width: _____

   b) Draw a diagram of your shape, and label it.

3. Find the area and the perimeter of your shape. Include the formula and the units of measurement.

4. Suppose you were going to paint your shape. What measurement would you need to know, the area or the perimeter? _____ Explain.

5. Suppose you were going to put trim around your shape. What measurement would you need to know, the area or the perimeter? _____ Explain.

6. List 3 occupations where finding the area and/or the perimeter of shapes would be important. Explain why you would need measurements to do this job.

   •   •   •

3.1

3.1C Area and Perimeter: Combined Shapes

A triangle is _____ of a rectangle. Try it for yourself.

Thus, the area of a triangle is _____ the area of a rectangle.

$A_{\text{triangle}} =$

Practice

1. Find the area of each triangle.

   a) $A =$

   $=$

   $=$ 8 cm

   10 cm

   b) $A =$

   $=$

   $=$

   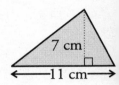

   7 cm

   ←—11 cm—→

2. Divide each shape into rectangles and triangles, and find the total area of the shape.

   a)

   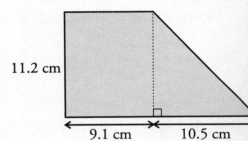

   11.2 cm

   9.1 cm   10.5 cm

   b)

   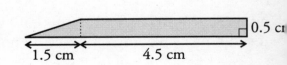

   0.5 cm

   1.5 cm   4.5 cm

   c)

   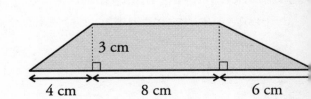

   3 cm

   4 cm   8 cm   6 cm

3.1D Area and Perimeter: Applications

When painting, wallpapering, or carpeting rooms, it is important to know the dimensions of the room. Explain.

. Lloyd is painting his family room.
Two walls are 3.5 m × 2.7 m, and the other two walls are
4 m × 2.7 m.

a) Draw a diagram for each wall, and find the total area of the walls.

b) A 4-L can of paint covers 20 m².
How many cans are needed to paint this room?

3.1

c) Each 4-L can of paint costs $32.95. Find the cost of the paint needed to paint this room. Be sure to include 15% for GST and PST.

d) Why might the number of cans of paint needed be more or less than your answer in b)?

2. Rhonda is replacing the flooring
   in her combined living room
   and dining room, as shown in
   the diagram.

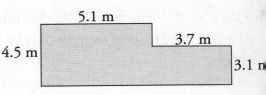

   a) Find the total area of the
   floor in both her rooms.

   b) Flooring comes in packages of 2 m².
   How many packages are needed?

   c) One package of flooring costs $49.95. How much will the
   flooring cost? (Include GST and PST.)

   d) Find the perimeter of the combined room.

   e) Baseboard molding for the edge of the floor comes in 3-m lengths.
   How many 3-m lengths will be needed?

   f) Why might she need more or less lengths of baseboard than she
   calculated in e)?

3. Suzy is wallpapering her bedroom. Each roll of wallpaper covers 12 m². Her room is square, and each wall is 10 m long and 3.1 m high.

a) How many rolls of wallpaper must she buy?

b) Each roll of wallpaper costs $19.95. What would be the cost for this wallpaper (including taxes)?

c) Why might the number of rolls needed be more or less than your answer in a)?

d) What are the advantages and disadvantages of painting and of wallpapering? Which method do you prefer and why?

3.1

4. Sandor's room is a **regular hexagon** as shown in the diagram. He is planning to carpet it. How many square metres of carpet will he need?

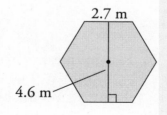

2.7 m

4.6 m

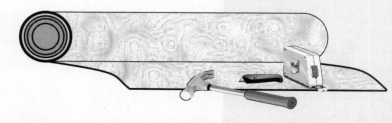

3.1E Area Assignment: Redecorate a Room

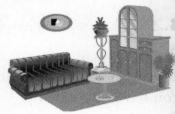

1. Choose a room in your home to paint or
   wallpaper and to replace the floor. What
   room did you choose?

   _____

2. Draw a diagram of the walls of this room, using a scale of your choice
   Include the dimensions of your room on the diagram. Use 1-cm graph
   paper. Attach diagram to assignment.

   Scale: 1 cm represents _____

3. Repeat question 2 for the floor.

4. Find out the price for a roll of wallpaper or a can of paint of your
   choice for the walls.
   a) Estimate how much material of your choice you will need, and
      estimate the total cost, including taxes.

   b) Calculate how much material of your choice you will need, and
      the total cost, including taxes.

5. Repeat question 4 for the flooring. (Consider carpeting or other floor
   covering.) You may need to complete this on a separate sheet of paper

3.1 Completed

Maximum Areas

3.2A A Swimmingly Great Problem

Problem

Your summer job includes roping off an area in a lake for swimming.
You have 60 m of rope, and you want the **greatest area possible** for
the swimmers. The area is to be rectangular, and the rope must fully
enclose the swimming area. What dimensions will make the greatest
swimming area?

Recall: perimeter, P, is distance around and area, A, is the amount of
surface area.

$$\text{Perimeter} = 2(\text{length}) + 2(\text{width}) \qquad \text{Area} = (\text{length})(\text{width})$$

Step 1 Make a Hypothesis

Make a hypothesis about the dimensions of the shape that will give the
maximum swimming area.

Step 2 Collect the Data

Explore the different possible shapes and the perimeter and area of each
shape.

a) You could rope off a long,
   narrow rectangular swim area
   like this.

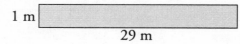

   1 m   29 m

   (i) Determine the perimeter of this swimming area.

   (ii) Determine the area of this swimming area.

b) You could rope off a rectangular shape
   like this that is wider and shorter than
   in a).

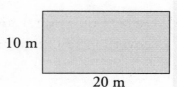

   10 m   20 m

   (i) Determine the perimeter of this
       swimming area.

   (ii) Determine the surface area of this swimming area.

Step 3 Organize the Data

2. Complete this chart to determine the areas for other possible rectangular shapes with perimeter 60 m.

Perimeter (m)	Length (m)	Width (m)	Area (m²)
60	30		
60	29	1	29
60	28		
	22		
	17		
	16		
	15		
	14		
	13		
	2		
	1		
	0		

Did you really need to complete the whole chart? Explain.

3. Present your data in the table from the previous page by making a scatter plot of length vs. area.
Be sure that the graph includes correct titles, units, and scale.

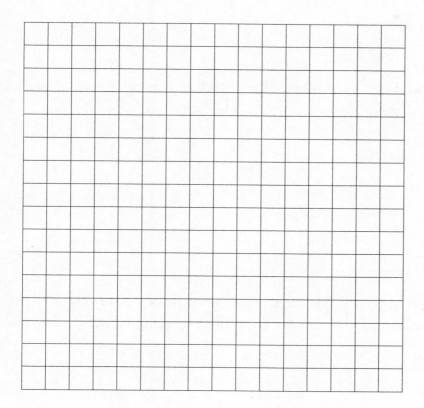

3.2

4. Draw the line (curve) of best fit.

Step 4 Make a Conclusion

5. Consider your data and the graph.

a) What dimensions would give the largest swimming area?

b) Draw a diagram and label it.

c) Explain your answer.

6. Check your hypothesis from Step 1. Was your hypothesis correct? Make any necessary changes.

7. If you were given 90 m of rope, what dimensions would give the largest area? Draw a diagram and label it.

8. What other things, besides the amount of swimming area, might need to be considered when roping off a rectangular area for swimmers?

3.2

3.2B Down the Garden Path: Maximum Area

The Problem

You are designing a garden. It is to be rectangular and to have a perimeter of 640 cm. You want to determine the dimensions of the garden that will give the maximum (largest) possible area.

1. Make a hypothesis about the best dimensions for the garden.

2. Collect the required data. Include well-labelled diagrams and computations. Use the grid on the following page.

   Helpful Notes:
   - Uni-cubes or grid paper may be used.
   - The formula for the perimeter of a rectangle is $P = 2l + 2w$.
   - The formula for the area of rectangle is $A = (l)(w)$.
   - For a given perimeter, (640 cm in this problem), once the length is chosen, the width is automatically determined.

   3.2

3. Organize the data collected in question 2 in the chart below.

Perimeter (m)	Length (m)	Width (m)	Area (m²)

4. a) Present your data from question 3 by making a scatter plot of length vs. area. Be sure that your graph includes titles with units, if necessary, and scales.

b) Draw the line (curve) of best fit.

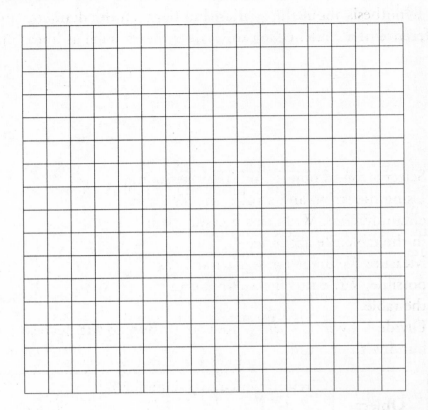

5. Make a recommendation about the best dimensions for this garden. Explain your answer.

6. Check your hypothesis with the graph. Adjust it if necessary.

7. What other items might need to be considered, besides the area, when building a garden?

3.2 Completed

Circles

3.3A Pi Development

Hypothesis

Make a hypothesis about the relationship between the **diameter** and the **circumference** of a circle. (Use proper descriptors, such as linear or non-linear.)

1. **a)** Select a round object from the classroom.
    b) Using the string and a ruler, measure the circumference. Write this measurement in the table. Be accurate.
    c) Measure the diameter as accurately as possible. Write this measurement in the table.
    d) Divide C by d ($C \div d$). Write your answer to the nearest hundredth of a unit.

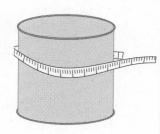

3.3

Object	Circumference (C)	Diameter (d)	$C \div d$

e) What appears to be true about the numbers in the final column?

_____

_____

2. a) Graph the data from the table in the previous page. Use the horizontal axis for the diameter and the vertical axis for the circumference.

   b) Make a scatter plot and draw the line of best fit.

3. Use your graph to determine the slope and y-intercept.

   slope, m = _____ y-intercept, b = _____

4. Write the equation of your line. _____

5. Conclusions:

   a) The slope of my line is an approximation for _____.

   b) This number is necessary when finding the area and

      perimeter of a _____.

   c) The formula for the circumference of a circle is _____.

   d) The formula for the area of a circle is _____.

3.3

3.3B Circle: Area and Circumference

Area of circle, $A =$ _____

Circumference of a circle, $C =$ _____

1. Find the area and the circumference of the circle.

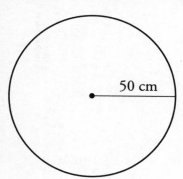

50 cm

$A = \pi r^2$

$C = \pi d$

2. a) Find the area and the circumference of the circle.

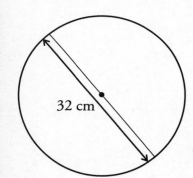

32 cm

$A = \pi r^2$

$C = \pi d$

3.3

b) Draw and label a diagram of half the circle in part a).
Find the area and perimeter of this semicircle.

3. Many signs are circular in shape. A town has 150 round signs each with a diameter of 40 cm.

a) The town is going to repaint all the signs. Why will the area of the circle need to be known?

b) Draw a diagram of one sign. Label it, and find its area.

c) A can of paint covers 15 m². How many cans of paint will be needed to paint all 150 signs?

3.3

4. Gene has a coffee table that is in the shape of a semicircle. Its diameter is 2.5 m.

a) Draw the top of Gene's table. Include the dimensions.

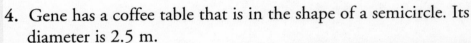

b) Gene wants to put a trim around the edge of this table. Use a coloured pencil on your diagram to show where the trim will go.

c) Find the amount of trim Gene needs to purchase.

5. A window is in the shape of a rectangle with a semicircle on top. The glass in the rectangular part is 24 cm along the top and 50 cm down the side.

a) Draw a diagram of the window and label it.

b) Find the amount of glass required for this window.

c) Find the length of trim needed to put around the outside of this window.

. Renata built a wooden play house for her children. One wall had two identical circular windows. What area of this wall needed paint?

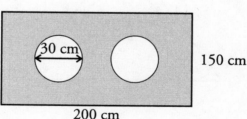

30 cm

150 cm

200 cm

   Area of painted region
= area of rectangle area − area of circular windows

=

=

3.3C Areas of Combined Shapes

Pair–Share: Partner A writes, and Partner B coaches.
                 Then, Partner B writes, and Partner A coaches.

1. Find the total area of this shape.

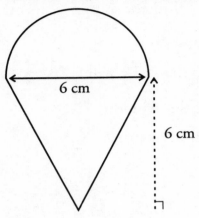

6 cm

6 cm

3.3

2. Find the shaded area.

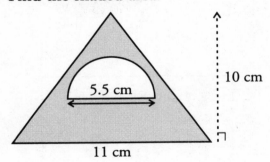

5.5 cm

10 cm

11 cm

Name _____   Date _____

3.3D Round and Round and Round . . .

Problem

Put a ring around the equator so that it fits snuggly, and there is no overlap. Then, increase the length of this string by 2 m.

Place this adjusted piece of string around the equator so that it sits out from the equator equally all around.

How far out from the equator do you think the string will be? The radius of Earth is about 6400 km.

Which of the following statements do you think is true?

a) A flea might squeeze under the string.

b) A mouse would brush its ears on the string.

c) A human could wriggle under the string.

d) You could drive a sports car under the string.

3.3

Use your skills with circumference to find the answer. Show all necessary work.

3.3 Completed

Pythagorean Theorem

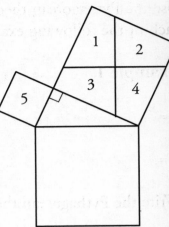

Use the Pythagorean Puzzle Master provided by your teacher, to complete this activity. Use the space below to construct your puzzle.

3.4A Pythagorean Theorem Puzzle

Cut out pieces 1, 2, 3, 4, and 5. Do not cut anywhere else. Place these pieces on the square on the hypotenuse of the triangle.
Make sure they fit exactly.
Glue them on.

Conclusion

In a right triangle, the sum of the areas of the _____

on the two adjacent sides is _____ to the area of the

_____ on the _____.

This can be written as $a^2 + b^2 = h^2$, where a and b represent the length of the two adjacent sides and h represents the length of the hypotenuse of the triangle.

3.4B Using the Pythagorean Theorem

Use the Pythagorean theorem to find the missing side of the triangle in each of the following examples.

Example 1

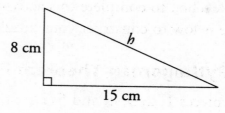

8 cm

h

15 cm

a =

b =

Write the Pythagorean theorem: $a^2 + b^2 = h^2$

Substitute. $8^2 + ($ $)^2 = h^2$

Solve for h. $= h^2$ **Note: What does a square root symbol $\sqrt{\ }$ mean?**

                                        $= h$

Example 2

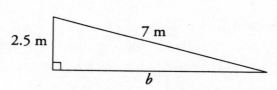

2.5 m

7 m

b

a =

b =

Write the Pythagorean theorem.

Substitute.

Solve for b.

3.4

Example 3

Find the length of the wheelchair ramp.

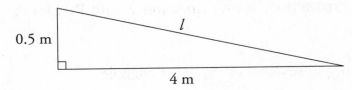

0.5 m

l

4 m

Estimate the answer first.

Write the Pythagorean theorem.

Substitute.

Solve for *l*.

Conclusion (Final Statement)

Example 4

A 3.5-m ladder is leaning against a wall.
The base of the ladder is 1 m from the wall.
How high up the wall does the top of the ladder reach?

Draw a diagram,
and label it.

Write the Pythagorean theorem.

Substitute.

Solve.

Conclusion (Final Statement)

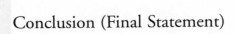

3.4C More Pythagoras

Pair–Share: Partner A writes for question 1, and Partner B coaches.
Then, Partner B writes for question 2, and Partner A coaches.

1. **a)** Find the missing dimension of the right triangle.
    b) Find the area.

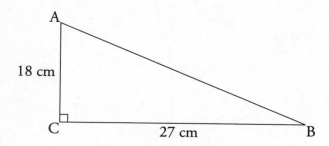

2. Use the diagram below to explain the Pythagorean theorem,
    $x^2 + y^2 = z^2$, in terms of the areas of squares on the sides of a
    right triangle.

3.4

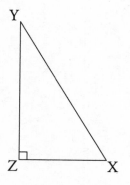

3.4 Completed

Three-Dimensional Geometry

3.5A Nets and Solids

a) Match each net in column 1 with a solid in column 2.

b) Match each solid in column 3 with a net in column 4.

3.5

1. Net	2. Solid	3. Solid	4. Net
a)	A.	a)	A.
	B.		B.
b)	C.	b)	C.
	D.		D.
c)	E.	c)	E.
			F.
d)	F.	d)	
	G.		G.
e)	H.	e)	H.
	I.		I.
f)	J.	f)	J.

3.5B Surface Area of Prisms

1. The diagrams of a solid and its
   net are given at the right.

   a) What type of solid is shown
      at the right?

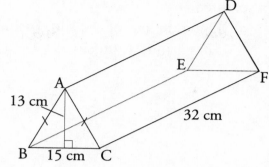

   b) Use the Pythagorean theorem
      to find the length of AC on
      the solid. Round your answer
      to the nearest whole centimetre.

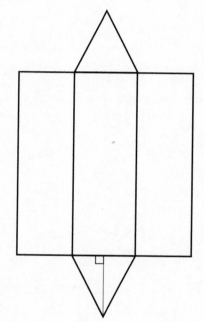

   c) Use the values given for the sides and
      the answer in part b) to label the net
      with the correct dimensions.

   d) Determine the total surface area of the solid.

   e) The material needed to cover this solid costs $0.25/cm². What is
      the cost of the material needed to cover this solid?

3.5

2. The top and sides of the silo shown need to be
painted.

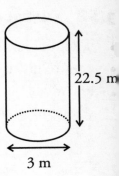

22.5 m

3 m

   a) Draw the net of the silo. Include as many
   dimensions as possible.

   b) Determine the total surface area that needs to be painted.

   c) A 4-L can of paint covers 40 m². Determine the number of cans of
   paint required to paint the silo.

   d) One can of paints costs $35. Find the total cost to paint this silo
   (including taxes).

3.5

3.5C Three-Dimensional Geometry: Surface Area

- A solid is given. Write in the name of the solid.
- Draw the net of each solid.
- Calculate the total surface area of the solid.

Name of Solid	Net of Solid Made Up of ___ ☐s + ___ ○s + ___ △s	Surface Area of Solid
12 cm, 3 cm, 5 cm		
10 cm, cm, 15 cm, 6 cm		
9 cm, 16 cm		
4 cm, 3 cm		

3.5D Volume of a Prism

The **volume** of a prism can be calculated using the formula:

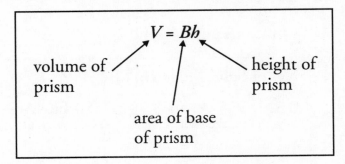

$$V = Bh$$

volume of prism

area of base of prism

height of prism

Find the volume of the solids in Examples 1 and 2.
Remember to write a final statement for your answer.

Example 1

Write the formula.

$V = Bh$ The base is a rectangle, so its
                  area is length times width.

$\quad = (l \times w)h$ Substitute the values of the
                  variables.

$\quad = ($ $)($ $)($ $)$

$\quad =$

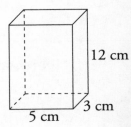

12 cm

3 cm

5 cm

Example 2

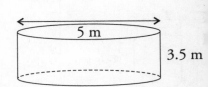

5 m

3.5 m

Write the formula.

$V = Bh$ The base is a circle so,
                  its area is _____.

$\quad = ($ $)($ $)$

$\quad =$

$\quad =$

3.5

3.5E Volume of a Pyramid

You will need
- one pyramid and one prism with the same height and identical (congruent) bases
- water, or rice, or any material that you can pour

Process

1. As a group, discuss what you think the relationship is, if any, between the volume of your pyramid and the volume of your prism. Write down your hypothesis.

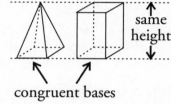

same height

congruent bases

2. Now fill your pyramid with one substance. The level at the top of your pyramid should be flat. Pour the substance from your pyramid into the prism. Repeat this until your prism is full and its contents are level at the top.

3. Count the number of filled pyramids you needed to fill your prism. Be as accurate as possible.

4. Repeat steps 2 and 3, using different material to fill your shapes.

Conclusion

1. Write in your own words, any relationship you found between the volume of your pyramid and the volume of your prism.

2. Recall the formula for the volume of a prism.
$V = Bh$ (This is read: The volume of a prism is equal to the area of its base times its height.)
Create a formula that relates the volume of a prism to the volume of a pyramid. Write it in formula form and in words.

3.5

3.5F Minimum Surface Area: Rectangular Prism

Activity

Construct a rectangular prism that has a volume of 64 cm³ and that has the smallest (minimum) surface area.

Materials

Each group will need 64 unit cubes.

Instructions

Your group has 64 unit cubes. Many different rectangular prisms can be made with these cubes. All of them will have a volume of 64 cm³. Will all of them have the same surface area?

Make a hypothesis about the dimensions of the prism with the minimum surface area.

1. Gather data.

Area of Base (length)(width)	Height	Surface Area	Volume
(1)(1) = 1	64	(64)(1)(4) + (1)(1)2 = 258	64
(1)(4) = 4	16	(16)(4)(2) + (16)(1)(2) + (1)(4)(2) = 168	64
(2)(8) =		(8)(4)(2) + (2)(4)(2) + (2)(8)(2) =	
(2)(2) =			
(4)(4) =			
(8)(8) =			
(2)(32) =			
(2)(4) =			
(4)(16) =			
(1)(2) =			

2. Draw a scatter plot on the grid below, using the area of the base as the independent variable and the surface area as the dependent variable. (Plan your scale carefully by studying the chart.)

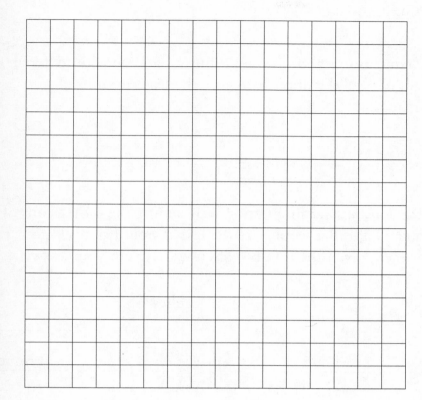

3. Conclusions: What are the dimensions of the prism that has a volume of 64 cm^3 and that has the least surface area? Explain.

4. What are the dimensions of the prism that has a volume of 64 cm^3 and that has the greatest surface area? Explain.

3.5

5. Can you think of any real life examples where knowing the minimum surface area for a given volume would be important? Explain why.

6. Using your conclusions above, when filling a package with material, which rectangular solid will probably use the least amount of packaging material?

7. Demonstrate your answer in question 6 by stating the dimensions of the rectangular solid that would use the least amount of packaging material for each, given the number of cubes. Explain your answer.

3.5

a) 8 cubes

b) 27 cubes

c) 48 cubes

d) 125 cubes

e) 60 cubes

8. Think of rectangular containers in the supermarket, such as juice boxes, cereal boxes, and cracker boxes.
   a) Do they approximate the shape that minimizes the surface area? Explain.

   b) Give reasons why you think some boxes that are constructed do not minimize their surface area?

.5G Surface Area and Volume of a Cylinder

. Take a rectangular piece of paper that is not square-shaped.
   Measure its length and its width.

Length: Width:

. Roll it into a tube.
   Do not overlap the edges of the paper.
   Tape the edges together.
   Sketch this tube, and insert its dimensions.

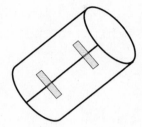

. Use your measurements from question 1 to find the surface area of
  the tube. Exclude the top and the bottom.

3.5

. **a)** Measure the radius of the base of your tube.

. **b)** Find the volume of your tube. Remember: The volume of a
     cylinder is found by multiplying the area of the base by the
     height.

5. Roll the paper in the other direction to make another tube.
   Do not overlap the paper.
   Sketch this tube, and put in its dimensions.

6. What is the surface area of the tube in question 5?

7. a) Measure the radius of the base of the tube in question 5.

    b) What is the volume of this tube?

3.5

8. Compare the volumes and the surface areas of the tubes you
   constructed.
   a) What results are the same? Explain.

   b) What results are different? Explain.

9. Consider your results in this section and in Section 3.5F. What
   dimensions of a cylinder do you think maximizes the volume for a
   given surface area? (Assume there is a top and a bottom.)

3.5 Completed

Relations in Euclidean Geometry

.6A Introduction to *The Geometer's Sketchpad®*

The Toolbox *(blue column on the left of the screen)*

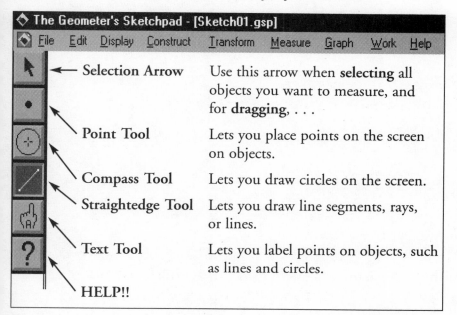

Selection Arrow	Use this arrow when **selecting** all objects you want to measure, and for **dragging**, . . .
Point Tool	Lets you place points on the screen on objects.
Compass Tool	Lets you draw circles on the screen.
Straightedge Tool	Lets you draw line segments, rays, or lines.
Text Tool	Lets you label points on objects, such as lines and circles.
HELP!!	

eat Things to Know

To clear the screen

To select several objects at once.

To draw horizontal and vertical lines

Practice

1. **a)** Draw 2 points, 2 line segments, 2 rays, 2 lines, and 2 circles.
    Then, label all the points created on your screen.
    Write a short description of what you observed or discovered.

    Now, clear the screen!!

    b) With your partner, create a grid for tick-tack-toe and play a
    game.

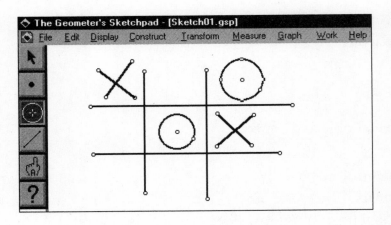

I Menus

Construct

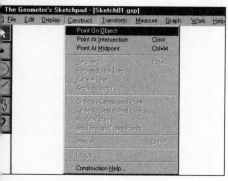

Measure

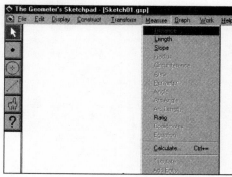

Practice

. Use the **Construct** menu and then, the **Measure** menu to complete each of the following. Include all necessary labels and dimensions.

a) line segment AB whose length is 4.4 cm

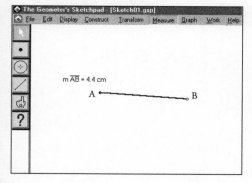

b) $\angle CDE = 20.7°$

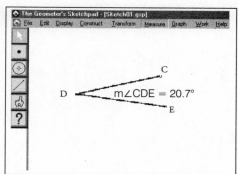

c) a polygon and the measure of its perimeter and area. It is necessary to Construct Polygon Interior. Then, drag a corner of the polygon. What happens to the measurements?

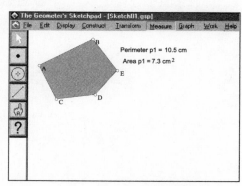

d) Construct a circle

Measure its circumference and area.

Drag the centre.

Drag the **handle**.

What happens to the measurements?

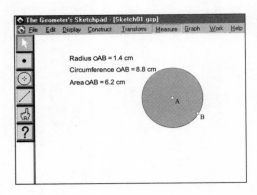

e) Construct parallel lines and perpendicular lines.

Drag each line. Are they still parallel or perpendicular?

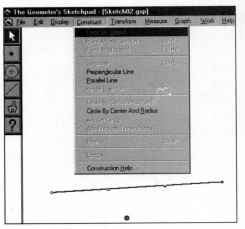
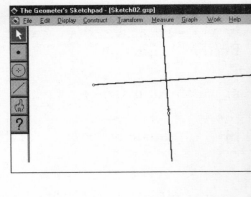

2. Create a picture using the constructions that you have learned.

II Pictures That Move

Animation

a) Using the **Compass** tool, draw a circle on the screen.
b) Select the circle and from the **Construct** menu select **Point On Object**.
c) Draw a line segment from this point, ending anywhere on the screen.

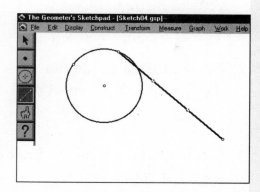

. Select the circle and the point on the circle at the same time. From the **Edit** menu select **Action Button, Animation**.

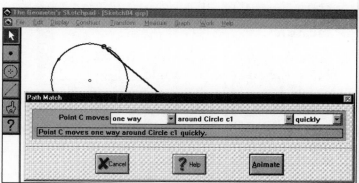

a) Select **Animate**.

b) An Animate box appears on the screen. Double click the Animate box.

c) Move the end of the segment inside the circle and animate.

d) Add several line segments, all ending on the circle.
Select the circle and all the endpoints on the circle at the same time.
From the **Edit** menu select **Action Button, Animation, Animate . . .**

. Now it's your turn.
Create a picture with circles, lines, points, and polygons.
Add a little colour and a lot of action . . .

3.6B The Sum of the Angles of a Polygon

Part 1 Triangles

1. Construct a triangle and label the vertices A, B, and C.

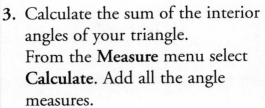

2. Measure all three interior angles of the triangle. (See section 3.6A.)

3. Calculate the sum of the interior angles of your triangle.
   From the **Measure** menu select **Calculate**. Add all the angle measures.

   State the sum of the angles. _____

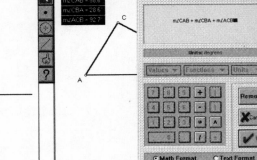

4. Drag one of the vertices of your triangle.

   State the sum of the angles. _____

   (Try animating your construction where one, or all, of the vertices moves along different paths.)

Observations

What happens to the measure of each angle of your triangle?

What happens to the sum of the angles of your triangle?

Conclusion

Part 2 Quadrilaterals

1. Construct a quadrilateral, and label the vertices as indicated.

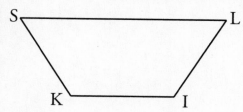

2. Measure each interior angle of your quadrilateral.

3. Calculate the sum of the interior angles of your quadrilateral.

State the sum of the angles. _____

4. Drag one of the vertices of your quadrilateral.

State the sum of the angles. _____
(Try animating your construction where one, or all, of the vertices move along different paths.)

Observations

What happens to the measure of each angle in your quadrilateral?

What happens to the sum of the measures of the angles in your quadrilateral?

Conclusion

3.6C The Sum of the Interior Angles of a Polygon: Activity

Part 1

1. **a)** Draw a quadrilateral in
        the space provided.

    b) Draw a **diagonal** in your quadrilateral above.
        How many triangles did you form? _____

    c) State the sum of the interior angles of a quadrilateral from
        Section 3.6B. _____
        Recall the sum of the angles of a triangle (ASTT).
        How is the number of triangles you formed related to the sum of
        the angles of your quadrilateral?

    d) How is the number of triangles you formed related to the
        number of sides of your quadrilateral?

2. **a)** Draw a **pentagon** in
        the space provided.

    b) Draw diagonals in your pentagon to form triangles.
        Do not have any of your diagonals crossing.
        How many triangles did you form? _____

    c) Use the number of triangles you formed and ASTT to find the
        sum of the interior angles of a pentagon. _____

    d) How is the number of triangles you formed related to the
        number of sides of the pentagon?

Part 2 Sum of the Interior Angles of a Polygon

Hypothesis

Make a hypothesis about the relationship between the number of sides of a polygon versus the sum of the interior angles. (Use proper descriptors, such as linear and non-linear.)

Instructions

Use the conclusions of Activity 3.6C, Part 1, to gather data on the sum of the interior angles of polygons up to octagons (8-sided).

Polygon and Number of Sides	Number of Triangles Formed by Diagonals	Sum of Interior Angles	First Differences
Triangle 3		180	
Quadrilateral 4	2		
Pentagon 5			
6			
7			
8			

What appears to be true about the first differences?

_____

What does this mean about the relationship between the number of sides of a polygon and the sum of the interior angles?

3.6

Using the data collected in the table on the previous page, construct a scatter plot of the number of sides versus the sum of the interior angles. Use the horizontal axis for the number of sides of the polygon and the vertical axis for the sum of the interior angles.

Scatter Plot and Line of Best Fit.
Remember to label the axes and graph.

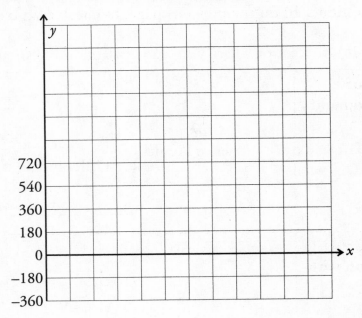

3.6

1. **a)** From your graph, determine the slope and y-intercept.

   Slope, $m =$_____ y-intercept, b = _____

   b) Write the equation of your line. _____

2. Extrapolate your graph to determine the sum of the interior angles of each polygon.

   a) a 9-sided polygon (nonagon)   _____

   b) an 11-sided polygon   _____

3. The sum of the measures of the angles of a polygon is 1440°. Using your graph, the polygon has _____ sides.

4. Explain why it is impossible for the sum of the interior angles of any polygon to be 1450°.

5. For your answers to each of the following in the table below, use your equation, from question 1 b) on the previous page, to check each of your answers.

sum of the interior angles of a polygon with 9 sides	
sum of the interior angles of a polygon with 11 sides	
number of sides in a polygon with an interior angle sum of 1440	

6. In your own words, make a conclusion about the sum of the interior angles of a polygon and the number of sides of the polygon.

3.6

3.6D Exterior Angles of a Polygon

Part 1 Triangles

1. a) Construct a triangle, using the **Segment** tool, and label all points as indicated.

    b) Construct $\overrightarrow{AB}$, $\overrightarrow{BC}$, and $\overrightarrow{CA}$, using the **Ray** tool.

    c) Construct points D, E, and F, as indicated.

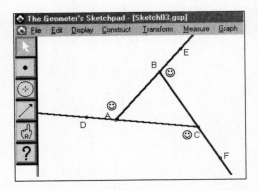

2. a) Measure the three indicated **exterior** angles of the triangle.

    b) Calculate the sum of the exterior angles of the triangle.

        The sum of the exterior angles is _____.

3. Drag one of the vertices of your triangle to a new position.

    The sum of the exterior angles is _____.

    (Try animating your construction where one, or all, of the vertices move along different paths.)

Observations

What happens to the measure of each of the exterior angles in the triangle?

What happens to the sum of the exterior angles of the triangle?

Conclusion

What appears to be true about the sum of the exterior angles of a triangle?

Part 2: Quadrilaterals

1. **a)** Construct a quadrilateral using the **Segment** tool, and label all points as indicated.

    b) Construct $\overrightarrow{AB}$, $\overrightarrow{BC}$, $\overrightarrow{CD}$, and $\overrightarrow{DA}$ using the **Ray** tool.

    c) Construct points E, F, G, and H as indicated.

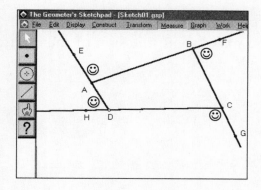

2. **a)** Measure the four indicated exterior angles of the quadrilateral.

    b) Calculate the sum of the exterior angles of the quadrilateral.

    The sum of the exterior angles is _____.

3. Drag one (or more) of the vertices of your quadrilateral to a new position. (Try animating your construction where one, or all, of the vertices move along different paths.)

    The sum of the exterior angles is _____.

Observations

What happens to the measure of each of the exterior angles in the quadrilateral?

What happens to the sum of the exterior angles of the quadrilateral?

Conclusion

What appears to be true about the sum of the exterior angles of a quadrilateral?

3.6

4. a) Repeat question 1 for a pentagon or a hexagon.
    b) What conclusion can you make about the sum of the exterior angles of a pentagon or hexagon?

Conclusion

Describe in your own words what appears to be true about the sum of the exterior angles of any polygon.

3.6E Using Dynamic Geometry to "Prove" Geometric Theorems: Angles

1. Use *The Geometer's Sketchpad*® to draw each diagram shown. Label your diagrams using letters of your choice, unless otherwise indicated. You may use text and other resources to help you draw the diagram.
2. Measure the indicated sides, angles, etc. Observe the results.
3. State your conclusions.
4. Check your results; then, complete the practice questions.

Theorem/ Property	Diagram	Measure/ Calculate	Observe	Conclusion
Complementary Angles (CA)	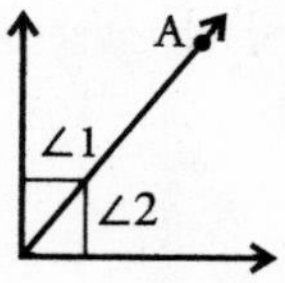	$\angle 1 =$ $\angle 2 =$ $\angle 1 + \angle 2 =$	Drag point **A**. What happens to the calculations?	
Supplementary Angles (SA)	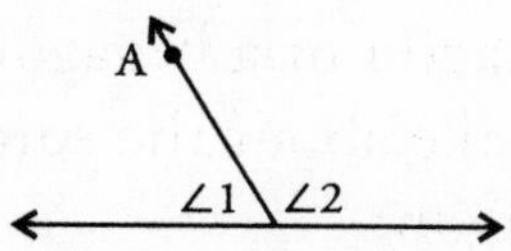	$\angle 1 =$ $\angle 2 =$ $\angle 1 + \angle 2 =$	Drag point **A**. What happens to the calculations?	
Opposite Angle Theorem (OAT)	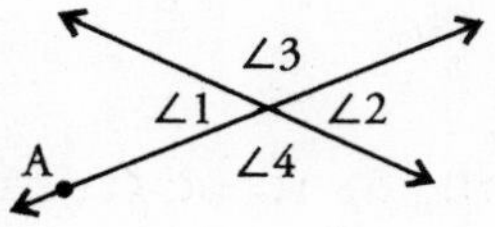	$\angle 1 =$ $\angle 2 =$ $\angle 3 =$ $\angle 4 =$	Drag point **A**. What happens to the calculations?	
Angle Sum Triangle Theorem (ASTT)	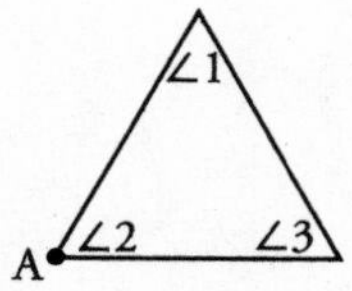	$\angle 1 =$ $\angle 2 =$ $\angle 3 =$ $\angle 1 + \angle 2 + \angle 3 =$	Drag point **A**. What happens to the calculations?	

3.6

Practice

1. Find the value of each variable and the measure of each angle.
   State the property or the theorem you used.
   Show your work.

a)

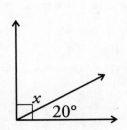

b)

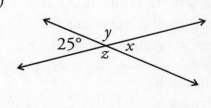

c)

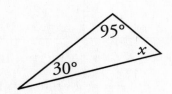

d)

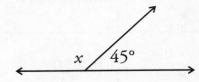

e)

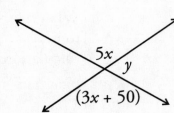

f)

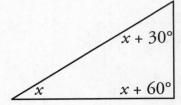

3.6

3.6F Using Dynamic Geometry to Prove Geometric Theorems: Parallel Lines

1. Use *The Geometer's Sketchpad*® to draw each diagram shown. Label your diagrams using letters of your choice, unless otherwise indicated. You may use text and other resources to help you draw the diagram.
2. Measure the indicated angles, etc. Observe the results.
3. State your conclusions.
4. Check your results; then, complete the practice questions.

Theorem or Property	Diagram	Measure or Calculate	Observe	Conclusion
Transversal Parallel Theorem (Alternate Angles) (TPT Z)	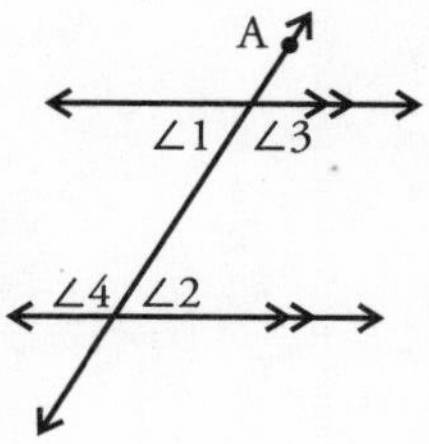 A	$\angle 1 =$ $\angle 2 =$ $\angle 3 =$ $\angle 4 =$	Drag point A. What happens to the calculations?	
Transversal Parallel Theorem (Corresponding Angles) (TPT F)	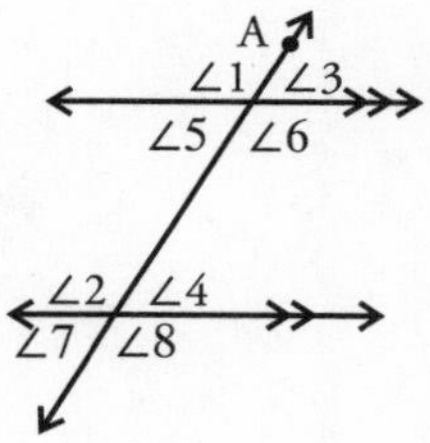 A	$\angle 1 = \quad \angle 2 =$ $\angle 3 = \quad \angle 4 =$ $\angle 5 = \quad \angle 7 =$ $\angle 6 = \quad \angle 8 =$	Drag point A. What happens to the calculations?	
Transversal Parallel Theorem (Interior Angles) (TPT C)	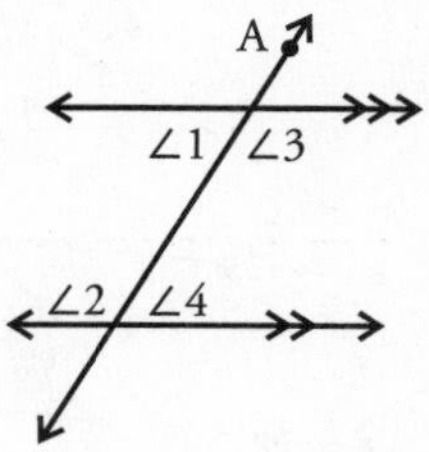 A	$\angle 1 =$ $\angle 2 =$ $\angle 1 + \angle 2 =$ $\angle 3 =$ $\angle 4 =$ $\angle 3 + \angle 4 =$	Drag point A. What happens to the calculations?	

3.6

Practice

1. Find the value of each variable and the measure of each angle.
   State the property or theorem you used.
   Show your work.

a)

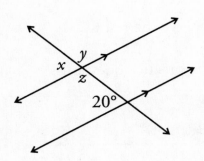

b)

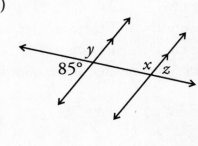

c)

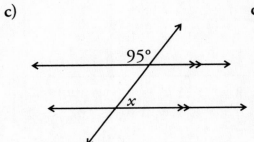

d)

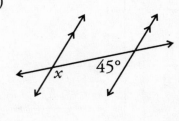

e)

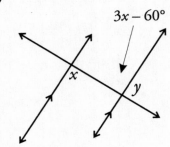

f)

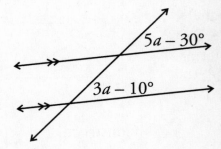

3.6G Using Dynamic Geometry to Look at Quadrilaterals

1. Use *The Geometer's Sketchpad*® to draw each diagram shown. Label your diagrams using letters of your choice, unless otherwise indicated. You may use text and other resources to help you draw the diagram.
2. Measure the indicated angles, etc. Observe the results.
3. State conclusions.
4. Check your results; then, complete the practice questions.

Theorem or Property	Diagram	Measure or Calculate	Observe	Conclusion
Interior Angles of a Quadrilateral	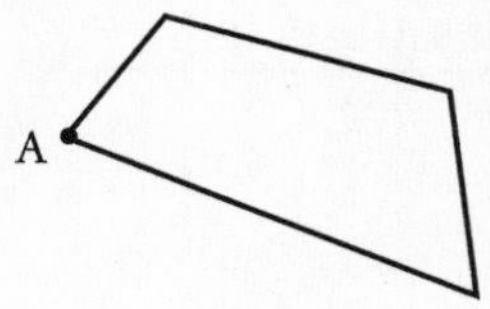 A	Measure the interior angles and find the sum.	Drag point **A**. What happens to your calculations?	
Exterior Angles of a Triangle	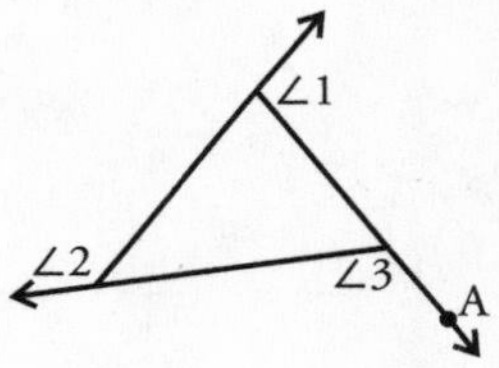 ∠1 ∠2 ∠3 A	Measure the 3 exterior angles and find the sum.	Drag point **A**. What happens to your calculations?	
Exterior Angles of a Quadrilateral	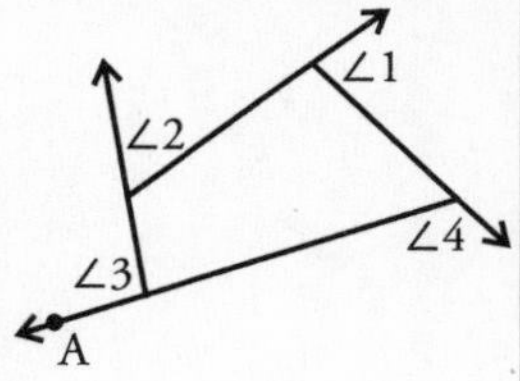 ∠1 ∠2 ∠4 ∠3 A	Measure the 4 exterior angles and find their sum.	Drag point **A**. What happens to your calculations?	
Diagonals of a Rectangle	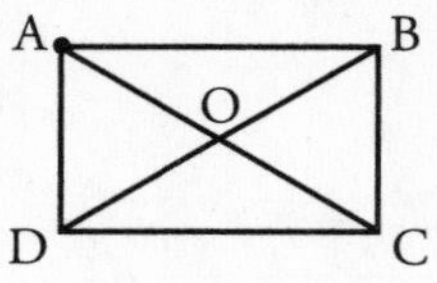 A B O D C Construct a rectangle and its diagonals that intersect at O, the point of intersection.	AC = BD = AO = CO = BO = DO =	Drag point **A**. What happens to your calculations?	

3.6

Theorem or Property	Diagram	Measure or Calculate	Observe	Conclusion
Diagonals of a Square	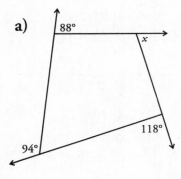 Construct a square and its diagonals that intersect at O.	Drag **A** until the 4 sides are the same. AB = BC = CD = DA =	Measure the angles. ∠AOB = ∠BOC = ∠COD = ∠DOA = Drag **A**. Ensure the 4 sides are the same. Do these angles change?	

Practice

3.6

1. Find the value of *x* and the measure of each angle.
   State the property you used.
   Show your work.

a) 88° *x* 118° 94°

b)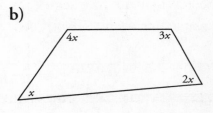

c) *x*

d)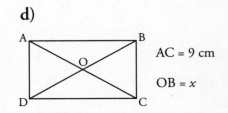
AC = 9 cm
OB = *x*

3.6H Circumcentre of a Triangle

1. Construct a **perpendicular bisector** of a line segment.

   a) Construct a segment.

   b) Select the segment and from the **Construct** menu select **Point at Midpoint**.

   c) Select the segment and the midpoint at the same time.
   From the **Construct** menu select **Perpendicular Line** (as in Activity 3.6A on page 170 of this text).

   d) Indicate the equal segments and the right angle on the diagram.

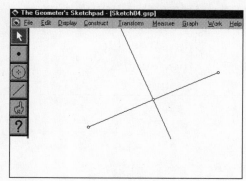

2. a) Construct a triangle as indicated.

   b) Construct the perpendicular bisector of each of the three sides.

   c) Select 2 of the line segments at the same time, and from the **Construct** menu select **Point at Intersection** and label it O.

   Point O is called the _____ of the triangle.

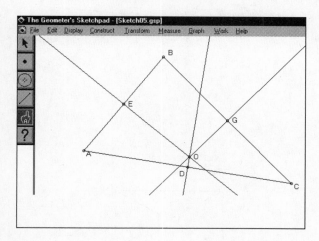

3.6

Circumscribing a Triangle

1. Select centre O and one of the vertices of the triangle at the same time.

2. From the **Construct** menu select **Circle by Center and Point.**

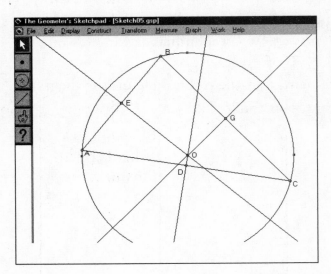

Conclusions/Observations

3.6I Triangle Centres and Their Properties

1. Use *The Geometer's Sketchpad®* to draw the diagrams shown. Label, using letters of your choice, unless otherwise indicated. You may use text and other resources to help you draw the diagram.
2. Measure the indicated angles, lengths, etc. Observe the results.
3. State your conclusions.
4. Check your results; then, complete the summary.

Theorem or Property	Diagram	Measure or Calculate	Observe	Conclusion
The **Centroid** of a Triangle	Construct ΔABC and the 3 **medians**. They intersect at O which is called the **centroid**.	AO = OF= $\dfrac{AO}{OF}$ = BO = OE= $\dfrac{BO}{OE}$ = CO = OD= $\dfrac{CO}{OD}$ =	Drag point **A**. What happens to your ratios?	
The **Incentre** of a Triangle	Construct a triangle and its 3 angle bisectors. They intersect at O which is called the **incentre**.	Make the largest possible circle that stays inside the triangle, using O for the circle's centre.	Drag point **A**. Using the "handle" of the circle, resize the circle to just touch each side of the triangle. Can this always be done for a variety of traingles? Do you see why this point is called the **incentre**?	

3.6

Theorem or Property	Diagram	Measure or Calculate	Observe	Conclusion
The **Orthocentre** of a Triangle	*(diagram: triangle ABC with 3 altitudes intersecting at O)* Construct a triangle and its **3 altitudes**. They intersect at O, which is called the **orthocentre**.	Drag point **A**. Observe what happens to your **orthocentre**.	When is the **orthocentre** inside the triangle and when is it outside the triangle?	
The **Circumcentre** of a Triangle (as in Activity 3.6H)	*(diagram: triangle with vertices A, B, C and points E, F, D, O; perpendicular bisectors)* Construct a triangle and the perpendicular bisectors of all three sides. They intersect at O, which is called the **circumcentre**.	Drag point **A**. Observe what happens to your **circumcentre**.	When is the **circumcentre** inside the triangle and when is it outside the triangle?	

3.6

Summary

State the 4 triangle centres.

State one or more special properties of each centre.

-

-

-

-

3.6 Completed

Relations and *The Geometer's Sketchpad*®

3.7A Pi Demonstration (Again)

1. Construct a circle.
2. Construct the circle's diameter using the segment tool.
3. Measure the circumference.
   Select the circumference. Then, from the **Measure** menu, choose **Circumference**.
4. Measure the diameter.
   Select the diameter. Then, from the **Measure** menu, choose **Length**.

5. Calculate the circumference divided by the diameter.
   From the **Measure** menu select **Calculate**.
   Select the circumference from your screen, divide(/) from the calculator screen and then, the diameter from your screen.
   Finally, choose **OK**.

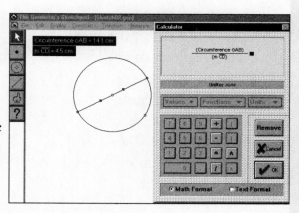

3.7

6. Drag the **control point** of the circle.
   Change the size of your circle and adjust the diameter for each new circle. Stop 4 times and record the data in your chart.

Diameter	Circumference	Ratio	$\dfrac{\text{Circumference}}{\text{Diameter}}$

Conclusion

Refer to Activity 3.3A on page 143 of this text. You now have completed the same activity on *The Geometer's Sketchpad*®.

3.7B The Pythagorean Theorem Using *The Geometer's Sketchpad*®

1. Construct right triangle ABC in the following way.
   - Construct a line segment AB.
   - Select line segment AB and point B at the same time.
   - Construct a line perpendicular to AB through B.
   - Place point C on the perpendicular line and construct segment AC (AC is the **hypotenuse**).
   - Select the perpendicular line. From the **Display** menu select **Hide**.
   - Construct segment BC.

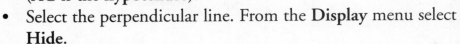

2. Measure AB and BC.
3. Calculate AB^2 (AB*AB) and BC^2 (BC*BC).
4. Calculate the sum of the squares of AB and BC. (AB*AB) + (BC*BC).
5. From the **Measure** menu select **Length**. Measure AC. Calculate AC^2 (AC*AC)(the hypotenuse).
6. Complete the following chart for several positions of point A.

$(AB)^2 + (BC)^2$	$(AC)^2$	Observations

7. Drag point C into different positions (or animate slowly). Does your observation hold true?

8. Restate the Pythagorean theorem.

3.7C Equations of Lines and *The Geometer's Sketchpad*®

1. From the **Graph** menu choose **Show Grid**.

2. Use your **Line** tool to construct any line.

3. From the **Measure** menu select **Slope**.

4. From the **Measure** menu select **Equation**.

   State the equation. _____

5. Select a point on the line and rotate it.

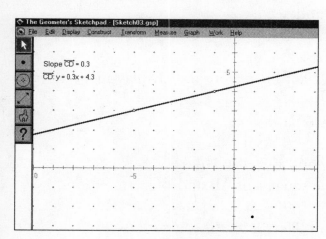

Stop and write the equation of the new line with

- a positive slope   Equation _____

- a negative slope   Equation _____

- a horizontal line   Equation _____

- a vertical line   Equation _____

3.7

3.7D Family of Lines: Activity

1. From the **Graph** menu select **Show Grid**.

2. Using the **Point** tool, place points at the coordinates (1, 2) and (−1, 6). Select the two points, and from the **Construct** menu choose **Line**. Calculate the slope of your line. (Remember the staircase.)

   $m =$ _____

   State the y-intercept. _____

   State the equation of your line. _____

   Check your equation from the **Measure** menu.
   Were you correct?

3. Drag the point (−1, 6) until it is on the y-axis.

   State the equation of your line. _____

   Drag the point (1, 2), and observe the corresponding equations.

   What do you observe about the equations? For example,

   • what changes?

   • what stays the same?

3.7 Completed

Name _____   Date _____

These awards are to help you keep track of your successes in the grade 9
applied course. Your teacher will instruct you as to how you will use
them. Keep up the good work.

Congratulations

3.1 Completed on
_____

Signatures_____
_____

Comments:

Achievement:
Thinking/Inquiry: 1, 2, 3, 4, NA
Communication: 1, 2, 3, 4, NA
Knowledge: 1, 2, 3, 4, NA
Application: 1, 2, 3, 4, NA

Congratulations

3.2 Completed on
_____

Signatures_____
_____

Comments:

Achievement:
Thinking/Inquiry: 1, 2, 3, 4, NA
Communication: 1, 2, 3, 4, NA
Knowledge: 1, 2, 3, 4, NA
Application: 1, 2, 3, 4, NA

UNIT

3

Congratulations

3.3 Completed on
_____

Signatures_____
_____

Comments:

Achievement:
Thinking/Inquiry: 1, 2, 3, 4, NA
Communication: 1, 2, 3, 4, NA
Knowledge: 1, 2, 3, 4, NA
Application: 1, 2, 3, 4, NA

Congratulations

3.4 Completed on
_____

Signatures_____
_____

Comments:

Achievement:
Thinking/Inquiry: 1, 2, 3, 4, NA
Communication: 1, 2, 3, 4, NA
Knowledge: 1, 2, 3, 4, NA
Application: 1, 2, 3, 4, NA

Congratulations

3.5 Completed on

_____

Signatures_____

_____

Comments:

Achievement:
Thinking/Inquiry: 1, 2, 3, 4, NA
Communication: 1, 2, 3, 4, NA
Knowledge: 1, 2, 3, 4, NA
Application: 1, 2, 3, 4, NA

Congratulations

3.6 Completed on

_____

Signatures_____

_____

Comments:

Achievement:
Thinking/Inquiry: 1, 2, 3, 4, NA
Communication: 1, 2, 3, 4, NA
Knowledge: 1, 2, 3, 4, NA
Application: 1, 2, 3, 4, NA

UNIT 3

Congratulations

3.7 Completed on

_____

Signatures_____

_____

Comments:

Achievement:
Thinking/Inquiry: 1, 2, 3, 4, NA
Communication: 1, 2, 3, 4, NA
Knowledge: 1, 2, 3, 4, NA
Application: 1, 2, 3, 4, NA